CPSIA information can be obtained
at www.ICGtesting.com
Printed in the USA
BVHW052302301121
622870BV00003B/263

Queen Victoria

A Captivating Guide to the Queen of the United Kingdoms of Great Britain and Ireland along with Her Impact on the Victorian Era

© Copyright 2021

All Rights Reserved. No part of this book may be reproduced in any form without permission in writing from the author. Reviewers may quote brief passages in reviews.

Disclaimer: No part of this publication may be reproduced or transmitted in any form or by any means, mechanical or electronic, including photocopying or recording, or by any information storage and retrieval system, or transmitted by email without permission in writing from the publisher.

While all attempts have been made to verify the information provided in this publication, neither the author nor the publisher assumes any responsibility for errors, omissions or contrary interpretations of the subject matter herein.

This book is for entertainment purposes only. The views expressed are those of the author alone, and should not be taken as expert instruction or commands. The reader is responsible for his or her own actions.

Adherence to all applicable laws and regulations, including international, federal, state and local laws governing professional licensing, business practices, advertising and all other aspects of doing business in the US, Canada, UK or any other jurisdiction is the sole responsibility of the purchaser or reader.

Neither the author nor the publisher assumes any responsibility or liability whatsoever on the behalf of the purchaser or reader of these materials. Any perceived slight of any individual or organization is purely unintentional.

Free Bonus from Captivating History
(Available for a Limited time)

Hi History Lovers!

Now you have a chance to join our exclusive history list so you can get your first history ebook for free as well as discounts and a potential to get more history books for free! Simply visit the link below to join.

Captivatinghistory.com/ebook

Also, make sure to follow us on Facebook, Twitter and Youtube by searching for Captivating History.

Contents

Introduction: The Hope for a Better Tomorrow

Even among kings and queens, there are very few that have an entire era named after them. Queen Victoria left such an impact on the world that her life and reign, which stretched from the early 1800s to the dawning of the 1900s, is widely known as the Victorian era. Houses are even named after this great monarch. If you live in the United Kingdom or any former British colony, you more than likely have seen an old Victorian home.

Such things stand as an ever-present testimony of just how much of a stamp Victoria has left on the world. The fact that a whole epoch of time was named after her shows just how lasting her legacy really was. Victoria's reign marked a period of great modernization and change, not just in Great Britain but also in the entire world.

During Victoria's time, inventions such as the telegraph, train, and photography were first made possible. And although these things do not even hold a candle to the internet, hypersonic planes, or the multimedia of today, they were indeed stunning achievements during Victoria's time. When she was born in 1819, the fastest anyone could go was dictated by the muscles of a horse's legs and the endurance in the animal's lungs.

By the end of her reign, however, it was possible to regularly travel across steel rails at speeds of up to eighty miles an hour, sustained not by the endurance of a horse but through the coal-fed engine of a locomotive. This meant that breaking news headlines on freshly printed newspapers could be loaded onto a cargo train and distributed far and wide. Of course, this was not as fast as scrolling through headlines on your phone minutes after they were written, but it was still quite revolutionary for the 19th century.

And with these changing times came changing attitudes. People began to question the "ancient regime" and seek new means of governance and representation. The role of kings and queens in England, which had its roots in absolute monarchy, had been slowly losing power for centuries. Throughout the years, the monarchy had been made to give increasing concessions, starting all the way back to the days of the Magna Carta, the royal charter forced upon King John in 1215.

It could be said that King George III—Victoria's own grandfather— was perhaps the last British king to wield real power. This king seemed to seal his fate after the disastrous loss of the American colonies, however, which his own policies of taxation had in large part brought about.

And by the time his several grown sons (who remained childless) reached the throne, one after another, the public had an increasingly dim view of the monarchy. It was universally viewed as a bastion of corruption, greed, and immorality. Some even openly wondered if it was time to abolish the institution outright.

It was only when Victoria took the throne after the last of her uncles had perished that the British people began to see the role of their monarch differently. Seeing this young, intelligent, and seemingly virtuous woman take the throne instilled the British people with pride. She seemed to represent the best that Britain had to offer. In her, they saw a little bit of themselves, and through her, they hoped for a better tomorrow.

Chapter 1 – The Fate of the Empire Depends on It

"Since it has pleased Providence to place me in this station, I shall do my utmost to fulfil my duty towards my country; I am very young and perhaps in many, though not all things—inexperienced. But I am sure that very few have more real good will and more real desire to do what is fit and right than I have."

-Queen Victoria

Victoria was born on May 24th, 1819, to her father, Prince Edward, and her mother, Princess Victoria of Saxe-Coburg-Saalfeld. Edward's wife Victoria had previously been married to a German prince named Charles (Emich Carl), Prince of Leiningen. She had two children with Charles—a boy named Carl and a girl named Feodora—before Charles abruptly passed away in 1814.

The newborn Victoria would take her name from her mother, Victoria of Saxe-Coburg-Saalfeld. Initially, however, her father, Prince Edward, had named her Alexandrina. This name was given in honor of one of the most powerful monarchs of the time—Tsar Alexander I of Russia.

Prince Edward was one of the younger sons of King George III. King George III had been declared incompetent at the time of Victoria's birth, and he would perish the following year (as would Victoria's father, Prince Edward, who died six days before his father). During this ordeal, his eldest son—Edward's older brother, who was also named George—was the acting king, reigning as prince regent. Since the younger George IV had no children of his own, the door was open that, someday, this baby girl might sit on the throne. It was with these considerations in mind that Edward's older brother wished that the newborn be named after him. He wished for her to be called Georgiana. When Edward's older brother told him of his wishes, Prince Edward was determined to name the child Alexandrina Georgiana.

But George did not like this since he felt that his name, being second to that of Alexander's, made him almost seem subservient to the Russian tsar. George is actually said to have declared, "No niece of mine shall put my name second to any king or emperor here in my own country. Call her Alexandrina Alexandra Alexander, if you choose, but she'll not be called Alexandrina Georgiana."

So, it was that the little princess was named Alexandrina Victoria instead, with the name Victoria being given, of course, in honor of her mother. But for those who knew and loved her at this stage in her life, she would be known simply as little Drina.

There was considerable question at the time as to who would ultimately hold the British throne. After King George III's death, his son, George IV, who had already been ruling as prince regent, was made king. George IV's only child, Princess Charlotte, had tragically passed away in 1817, just a couple of years before Victoria was born. This meant that Victoria was left as the only legitimate grandchild of George III, making her the potential future heir to the throne.

George IV would ultimately reign until he died in 1830. He was then succeeded by his next youngest brother, William IV. William IV died in 1837, and by that time, his only child had already perished,

leaving little Victoria as the ultimate successor of Britain's destiny. Out of all the possible outcomes of succession, it is said that this is the one that the British people had yearned for the most.

After all, Prince Edward had been looked upon favorably, and so had his little daughter Victoria. As rare as they may have been, the British people were known for having a fondness for female monarchs, such as the great Queen Elizabeth I, who reigned some two hundred years before Victoria was born. Thus, the British began to eagerly anticipate the crowning of their "little Princess."

This was something that Victoria's father had prepared for early on. It's said that when Victoria was only a few months old, he had taken her to inspect a detachment of British troops. When questioned as to why he brought a small child to such an engagement, the prince replied, "I want to see how she likes the army. You know she will be at the head of the army some day."

Not everyone was thrilled with Edward's enthusiasm at the time, though. In fact, it was none other than his older brother, Prince Regent George IV, who criticized the spectacle, declaring, "That infant is too young to be brought into public!" George IV was perhaps right in his estimation of events since, in those days, it was not uncommon for mere exposure to the elements to bring on severe illness. Actually, not long after this engagement, Prince Edward contracted a bad case of pneumonia from a different outing.

Upon examination by his doctor, Edward was found to be running a high fever, and it was the prevailing opinion of the physicians of the day that some blood must be drained from the patient in order to reduce it. After perhaps too much of this bloodletting, Prince Edward was a dead man. He passed away on January 23rd, 1820, leaving baby Victoria without a father.

Prince Edward's funeral was indeed a sad affair. Particularly touching was the moment Victoria, accompanied by her nurse, was seen by a crowd of mourners while she was seated in the back of a

carriage. As they were getting ready to leave, the nurse had the small child wave at the crowd. This sad sight stuck with the onlookers that day as they both mourned for Prince Edward and hoped for a brighter future with Victoria herself eventually on the throne.

For the time being, Victoria was dependent on her surviving parent: Princess Victoria of Saxe-Coburg-Saalfeld. She was a German princess, and there was some speculation that without her former husband to tie her to England, she might just pick up and move back to German lands. People wondered if she would end up in a Bavarian palace somewhere in Heidelberg, Germany, rather than the gloomy and depressing confines of a mourning Britain.

She had thought about it, but her brother, German Prince Leopold, who would eventually become the first king of the Belgians in 1831, convinced her to stay. He advised her that if her daughter should ultimately ascend to the British throne, it would be better if she grew up in England since, as he put it, "A Queen who has grown up in another country will never hold the hearts of the people."

His words were indeed wise, and his counsel was sound. Many times in the past when foreign monarchs had been placed on the English throne, English subjects did not take to them very well. King George I, for example, hailed from German-speaking lands, and for much of his reign, he spoke broken English. As such, his efforts to endear himself to the British were an uphill struggle.

Leopold would oftentimes be of considerable help to his sister Victoria and her namesake, baby Victoria, in their times of need. In fact, he would remain an unofficial adviser of sorts until he passed away in 1865.

Leopold had another tie to England besides his sister and niece. In 1816, he married King George IV's daughter, Princess Charlotte. After her sad passing in 1817, Leopold had made the fateful decision to stay in England. This proved to be quite providential for baby Victoria when her own father passed and the way began to be cleared

for her rise to the monarchy. For it was with the help of Leopold that room and board at the luxurious Kensington Palace were secured.

Fate can be a funny thing. And Leopold himself probably did not even fully realize the tremendous role he was playing. For it was upon little Victoria's uncle's broad shoulders and generous wallet that her successful upbringing—and, ultimately, the dynastic future of Britain itself—would come to depend.

Chapter 2 – Life at Kensington

"The greatest maxim of all is that children should be brought up as simply and in as domestic a way as possible, and that (not interfering with their lessons) they should be as much as possible with their parents, and learn to place the greatest confidence in them in all things."

-Queen Victoria

Little Victoria's daily routine at Kensington was a luxurious but straightforward affair with a quite rigid routine. Every day, she woke up and went to eat her morning meal at 8:00 a.m. sharp. During the course of the meal, Victoria would sit "in a tiny rosewood chair" right next to her mother.

It is said that her breakfast foods were not any more extravagant than what most other kids would have eaten at the time. Her morning meal typically consisted of just bread, milk, and perhaps a little fruit. It is said that her diet was kept plain on purpose so that she would not become too spoiled. She did have one particular extravagance that was granted her, however, in the form of a pretty white donkey. She would often take this beautiful beast of burden for a joy ride in the famed Kensington Gardens.

These forays would be followed by a light lunch, and then the child was allowed to go back out to play. Her day would usually end with a light supper, which, once again, consisted of mostly just bread and milk. She would then go to sleep in the room that she shared with her mother, ready to start it all over again upon waking the next day. When the child was around three years of age, her actual education began.

Her mother started off her curriculum like almost any other parent would—by teaching her daughter her ABCs. Victoria was not too keen about all of this at first since it cut into her playtime. What child would be, though, right? But despite her desire for a full day of play, the child was reasonable enough to reconsider. And once her mother explained how important the alphabet was since the alphabet would allow her to read books, Victoria promised to master the alphabet as quickly as she could.

And she did indeed learn the alphabet at a rapid pace, but once more rigorous learning materials were presented, she began to object once more. Her mother, feeling that she needed additional help in her daughter's education, just weeks before Victoria turned four years old, recruited a full-time tutor to teach her child. Her choice for the job was a man of the cloth, one Reverend George Davys, who hailed from a nearby church.

The lessons under Davys began that spring, with the reverend introducing the child to a box of alphabet blocks so that he could pick up right where Victoria's mother's training had left off. Soon, he had the girl working with letter combinations and finally simple words. Demonstrating just how sensitive she could be, when Davys had her spell out the word "b-a-d," she broke into tears. She apparently thought that the instructor was trying to suggest that she herself was being "bad." This would be comical if it wasn't so sad. The young girl obviously felt pressured to be at her best all the time, and she was already self-conscious that she was not stacking up.

Along with developing some sensitivities, she was also becoming a very honest child. Her mother would later recall how bluntly honest and candid little Princess Victoria could be. On one occasion, during a particularly difficult day with her daughter, she had scolded her, "Victoria, when you are naughty, you make both me and yourself very unhappy." To this, the girl honestly answered, "No, mamma—not me, but you." In other words, when she was acting out, it was only her mother that was upset since she herself usually enjoyed whatever mischief she had managed to get into.

There are those who would contend that Victoria would retain some of this candid nature for the rest of her life. She was most certainly frank and candid with her own future children, and a prime minister or two down the road might suggest as much from their later dealings with her as well.

At any rate, on her fourth birthday, the king of Great Britain, George IV, formally invited the princess to attend a special feast at the king's court. This was an early coming-out party of sorts for the princess. But despite the extravagance of the engagement, the invitation was mostly for show. After the princess was paraded around in front of the king and his cohorts and bid to say a few words, she wasn't allowed to stick around for the rest of the festivities. Instead, she was trundled off to go and dine on her usual diet of bread and milk. Nevertheless, even at this young age, Victoria was beginning to understand what was expected of her as a potential future head of state.

She also showed how much of an overachiever she was. Before her fifth birthday, when other children were struggling to even learn their alphabet, she had already learned to string together enough words to fire off a brief note to her instructor Reverend George Davys. She had been away with her mother on vacation when she sent the missive. The note read, "My dear sir I do not forget my letters nor will I forget you." This note was signed "Victoria," indicating that there was already a clear preference for that name over Alexandrina.

Her mother actually feared that the name Victoria might be a hindrance to the child since it was not too common in England at the time. The last thing she figured Victoria needed was to be pegged as a foreign usurper to the throne due to an unfamiliar first name. As fate would have it, the future Queen Victoria would make the name not only familiar to the English-speaking world but also quite popular. It is now hard to imagine Victoria seeming unfamiliar to the English tongue, and in modern parlance, it can be said to have a quintessentially British feel.

Back then, however, Victoria's mother was not quite so sure. Nevertheless, Victoria was generally well liked, and such concerns proved to be overblown. In fact, even King George IV eventually seemed to come around. Although he never really cared for the child's mother, he seemed to grow to genuinely like his niece. And one trip to the king's palace at the age of seven, in particular, was quite memorable.

At one point during her visit, King George IV had asked her to request his royal musicians to play a song, to which young Victoria is said to have responded, "I should like 'God Save the King.'" This, of course, is the British national anthem, which shifts from "King" to "Queen" when a female monarch is in power. The fact that little Victoria chose a song that requests God to put a special hedge of protection around the king (or queen) of Britain must have touched King George IV deeply.

Quite pleased with the child's mannerisms, he rewarded her a little later in the visit by taking her for a drive, in which King George himself was the driver, directing the team of horses as they took them about. Victoria recognized this special moment and was sure to mention it. In fact, right before she parted company with King George IV, he asked his niece what she enjoyed most while in his company. And without hesitation, she responded, "Oh, Uncle King, the drive I had with you."

It could be that the child was sincere in her musings, but some of the more cynical have noted that Victoria seemed to have already developed a keen mind for political strategizing. Young Victoria most certainly must have known that it was in her best interest to cultivate a strong relationship with her "Uncle King." Thus, some contend that all of this was merely pragmatic flattery on her part. If this really was the case, she was indeed a rather precocious and, yes, pragmatic seven-year-old child. Little Princess Victoria, it seems, knew full well that life at Kensington was not just about play but also practice for bigger things to come.

Chapter 3 – Growing up as the Future Queen

"You will find as the children grow up that as a rule, children are a bitter disappointment—their greatest object being to do precisely what their parents do not wish and have anxiously tried to prevent."

-Queen Victoria

In the year 1827, when she was around eight years of age, Victoria had a busy schedule. She was studying hard under her tutor, Reverend George Davys, who prepped and primed her on everything there was to know about the English language. Although her mother was a native German speaker, she had made sure that Victoria only spoke English in the home. Victoria was also being taught quite extensively in English history and the sciences. Some of the book titles that were on her shelf at the time were *An Introduction to Astronomy, Geography, and the Use of the Globes.*

It was probably best to keep Victoria busy during this period, for, that very year, her beloved older sister Feodora was married off to a German prince. This meant that Victoria would not be able to see her as often, which was a sad reality she had to accept. Nevertheless, the following year, in 1828, she made significant headway in her first

forays into academia, as she delved into religious studies, learned Latin, and discovered the catechism. It has been said, in fact, that she would devote no less than "one hour a week" in seeking to master the catechism.

And even when the week came to an end, the weekend didn't bring much relief to her studies either. Every single Saturday, when others were at rest, little Victoria was expected to deliver a personal report to her tutor, informing him of what kind of progress she had made during the week.

At the age of ten, however, Victoria saw some breakup of the monotony when she was invited to attend her first official ball. For those not familiar with the terminology, a ball was basically a festive yet formal kind of dance in which important people (typically royalty) were in attendance. Just think of Disney's *Cinderella* and the royal ball featured in the film, and you get the idea.

The king hosted the so-called Juvenile Ball or Children's Ball for both Princess Victoria as well as Maria II, the future queen of Portugal, who was barely a month older than Victoria herself. Maria just happened to be in England at the time, and the king apparently wanted to make the best of her visit by hosting a ball that would celebrate the young potentate.

During this occasion, Maria of Portugal was said to have been decked out in a stunning crimson velvet dress and bedecked with jewels. Little Victoria, however, sported a simple white dress. The two stood against a backdrop of well-dressed and well-heeled men and women. Victoria is said to have had a wonderful time, dancing and otherwise engaging in the festivities. For Maria II of Portugal, however, the night did not go quite so smoothly. At one point, she even fell and sustained an injury. Despite the immediate efforts to soothe her, she is said to have left the ball in tears. Although just a child, this could be considered an early lesson for Victoria on how important it was for royalty to be able to save face in public. Victoria herself would not always maintain a stiff upper lip during times of

hardship, but embarrassing incidents like this no doubt ingrained into her how important such things must be.

Soon after this event, when Princess Victoria was eleven years old, she was first made aware of the fact that she just might become Britain's queen. Her mom and namesake, Victoria of Saxe-Coburg-Saalfeld, had been carefully shielding her daughter from this possible eventuality. She did so in the hopes that she could prevent her daughter from becoming too proud at the thought that she might be queen.

Nevertheless, even without being told of the potential fate that awaited her, Victoria often wondered over the special deference that she was given. On one occasion, for example, when she was just a small child, she happened to notice the fact that grown-ups would often respectfully take off their hats when she approached them in public. The quick-minded Victoria noticed that this courtesy was done for her but not for her older half-sister, Princess Feodora.

Upon this realization, the inquisitive child is said to have asked her mother, "Mamma, why is it that when Feodora and I are walking all the gentlemen raise their hats to me and not to her?" Even at a young age, she knew that there was something different about her that held her apart from the others. But it was not until 1830, when she was eleven years old, that she finally received an explanation.

Around this time, King George IV had become deathly ill. Since King George did not have a direct heir, the only one left to succeed him was his brother, William. Upon becoming king, William would not have a direct heir either. And if William died without a direct heir, Victoria, as the grandchild of the former King George III, would be the next in line to the throne.

Since such a possibility seemed increasingly likely, Victoria was informed by both her mother and her tutors that she might expect to one day become the queen of Great Britain. Many believe, however, that at this point, it was more or less an open secret. Victoria was

certainly curious enough to put all of these puzzle pieces together ahead of time, so it is likely she must have known there was some possibility of such a thing occurring.

In later years, Victoria herself would suggest as much, stating that the knowledge of what she would one day become had slowly crystallized in her mind and filled her with both wonder and dread at the thought of the powerful position she would one day take. According to one account, the final realization of what awaited her came when her personal tutor, Reverend George Davys, gave her the assignment to compile a record of the kings and queens of England.

Victoria studiously did as was told, but her listing ended with the heir presumptive to George IV, which would have been her uncle, William. The tutor, however, wanted to see if Victoria would put herself in line after William. When asked who would come after William, an embarrassed Victoria explained, "I hardly liked to put down myself."

The princess was not too eager to take the throne. She knew that her road to being a queen was not going to be an easy one. It was deemed that should she become the heir, she would reign through an official regent until she turned eighteen years of age. This meant that until she came of age, her mother and advisers would hold more sway over her day-to-day decision-making than she would herself.

And in the lead-up to this process, one of the most important things for her to do was to take an exam before two bishops in order to prove that she was worthy of the task that lay before her. Her mother insisted that Victoria take a challenging examination to make sure that she had what it took to one day rule the British Empire. The bishops assigned with quizzing the youngster gave her a series of questions over Scripture, catechism, English history, Latin, and arithmetic.

Although the testing was rigorous, the two men were said to be gentle and kind with their approach. Just a few days later, the bishops who quizzed her sent the official results off to Princess Victoria's mom. The bishops stated that after asking Victoria a wide range of questions, she appeared to show an excellent comprehension of the material. Her examiners informed Victoria's mother that the girl was in excellent shape and well prepared to become Britain's next monarch. This was enough to convince Victoria's mother and her advisers that the young girl was on the road to success if they simply stayed the course.

Victoria turned eleven years old just a couple of months after this examination process, and just a short time after her eleventh birthday, King George IV perished, making her uncle William the new king (he would become known as William IV) and herself the runner-up to the throne.

In the meantime, the British Parliament had passed what was known as the Regency Act, which stipulated that if Victoria became queen prior to her age of majority (eighteen years of age), her mother would rule as regent in her stead.

There was still the possibility that William could have a child with his wife, Adelaide of Saxe-Meiningen, but as of yet, no such offspring had been produced, leaving Victoria in a category that was termed "heir presumptive." And she was indeed presumed to be the next in line to the throne unless the birth of a child between King William and Adelaide suddenly occurred.

Prior to marrying Adelaide, William had actually sired a whole string of children with former mistresses. But since these kids were all born out of wedlock and considered illegitimate, none of them had a legal claim to the throne. William had married the younger Adelaide later in his life, and it was unclear if he would have any legitimate children with his new bride. Ultimately, however, he would not, although Adelaide did give birth to several children, all of whom were either stillborn or died in infancy.

Victoria also became acquainted with the current queen, her aunt Adelaide. The child is said to have had a good relationship with her aunt, and on one occasion, they were both seen together standing from a palace window as a parade of well-wishers greeted them, cheering, "Hurrah for Queen Adelaide! Long live the Queen!"

It was then that Adelaide is said to have shown how magnanimous she was by bringing Victoria out to the edge of the balcony and presenting her to the crowd. The well-wishers saw young Victoria, and realizing that they were most likely looking at their future queen, they broke into cheers in her honor.

King William, Victoria's uncle, on the other hand, had a more complex relationship with the child. He is said to have genuinely liked his niece, but he had frosty relations with Victoria's mother. King William IV actually wished for Victoria to make more frequent court appearances in preparation for becoming queen, but Victoria's mother made sure to shield her daughter from court intrigue, stating that she was simply not ready "for the excitements of court life."

This show of restraint undoubtedly helped Victoria's mother maintain maximum influence on her daughter, whereas if she had assented to her being allowed at court, it would have been her uncle, King William IV, who would have been the most influential person in her life. William knew exactly what Victoria's mother was doing, and he resented her for it.

In the midst of all of this intrigue, in 1831, Princess Victoria's maternal grandmother, Victoria of Saxe-Coburg-Saalfeld's mother, passed away. Even though their visits were at times sporadic, Princess Victoria was close to her maternal grandmother, and she was deeply saddened by the loss.

That same year, she experienced another loss of another kind when her uncle Leopold was chosen to become the king of Belgium. True, her uncle was alive and well, but the fact that he was taking up such an important role would make him remote and nearly

impossible to reach. In the chessboard of Europe, in which borders were frequently in flux, Belgium had just become an independent nation in 1830. The new nation then had a big position to fill, and it sought out a potential king. Due to his family connections in the region and due to his powerful British connections, Leopold was ultimately selected to fulfill that role.

Incredibly enough, Leopold had just been offered to reign as king over the newly independent Greece, which had come to its own that same year, but he had refused. It is rare enough for a man to have the chance to be king fall into his lap one time, but good old Leopold apparently had the opportunity fall in his lap twice! Have you heard the old phrase "The third time's the charm?" Well, for dear Leopold, it was the second time around that was the charm, as he accepted Belgium's invitation to become king.

He would ultimately reign over the Belgians for the rest of his life, only stepping down by way of his own death in 1865. This meant that although one of Victoria's best allies was in a more powerful position, he was not going to be as available as he once was. The visit of a king, after all, had to be a highly orchestrated and arranged event. Her uncle could no longer drop by whenever he pleased. Life was changing for Victoria—and it would soon change even more.

In the years immediately prior to Queen Victoria taking the throne, her mother and attendants did everything they could to make sure that she was ready for the role that had been ordained for her. As a part of this preparation, they took Victoria on an extensive trip to oversee the land that she would soon be ruling. She did not get to travel the full extent of the British domain, of course, but she did get to see most of England, and she traveled all throughout the countryside on various vacation days that were set aside for her. She traveled both by train and by horse-drawn carriage. She naturally had an impressive entourage around her, as well as locals who requested the privilege to escort the presumptive heir around their villages.

King William was a bit derisive of the whole affair, likening it to a miniature version of the "great progressions" that Queen Elizabeth had made centuries prior, except he mocked the whole thing as being "little Victoria's royal progresses."

He was initially content to make fun of the whole affair, but eventually, the enthusiasm with which Victoria was met seemed to become a bit too much for him. And after noting that the navy was greeting Victoria with a formal gun salute, the king was not pleased. He immediately ordered those responsible to, as he put it, "Stop these poppings."

The British Royal Navy refused, however, stating that they were well within their rights and were simply adhering to tradition. The fact that the Royal Navy would openly go against a directive of the British king just goes to show how limited the monarch's powers already were on the very eve of Victoria's ascension to the throne.

Today, of course, the British royal family has been reduced to little more than figureheads. Back in King William's day, British kings and queens carried more power but were already being actively held in check by the British Parliament. At any rate, the Royal Navy did not "stop those poppings," no matter how much King William IV may have demanded that they do so.

Victoria was around thirteen years old at this point, and she was at an interesting crossroads in her life. Even while she was taking on more and more of the trappings of an important leader in Britain, she still enjoyed playing with dolls in her downtime. She was indeed still weening herself away from more childish things, and it is said that it was not until her fourteenth birthday that she finally decided to pack her dolls away and fully prepare herself for the next chapter of her life.

When Victoria was fourteen, King William held a ball in her honor, in which she was presented to all of the members of the court, and they vigorously drank to her health. Over the next few years,

Victoria would fluctuate back and forth between having the life of a young girl and that of a queen-to-be. It was in the middle of this transition, when Victoria was seventeen years old, that she first encountered Prince Albert.

Prince Albert was a first cousin from Victoria's mother's side of the family (his father was Victoria's mother's older brother). Although they were blood relatives, Victoria was quite smitten by her cousin. It was not at all uncommon in those days for members of royal families to marry their cousins since such a pairing was believed to quite literally "keep it in the family." At any rate, the two greatly enjoyed each other's company, and they became determined to see each other again.

In the meantime, Victoria was getting ever closer to that fateful day that she would become queen. Her destiny was all but sealed on May 24th, 1837, when she turned eighteen years of age. The following month, on June 20th, 1837, seventy-one-year-old King William IV passed away.

The timing of all of this allowed eighteen-year-old Victoria to immediately become queen, with an official regency no longer needed. This was something for which William himself had hoped. At a state dinner a few months prior to his death, when Victoria was still only seventeen, he even voiced his desire to have her take over immediately upon his demise without any need for a regency. In a moving message at the engagement, he announced to all assembled, "I hope that my life may be spared nine months longer, after which period, in event of my death, no regency will take place. I shall then have the satisfaction of leaving the royal authority to the personal exercise of that young lady"—here, the king looked at Princess Victoria and then, glaring at Duchess Victoria, he roared—"and not in the hands of a person now near to me."

The king is then said to have gone on a full-blown rant over the perceived grievances he had with Victoria's mother. Victoria's mother took these harsh words fairly well for her part, choosing to ignore

them in silence. Victoria, however, was not able to tune them out so well, and she broke down and cried right then and there. At the end of the festivities, it was customary for guests to spend the night. But after what they had gone through, Victoria and her mother were not too keen on a slumber party.

Nevertheless, Queen Adelaide, feeling bad about what had happened, intervened to stop them. She is said to have called out to them, "Stay—stay, I beg of you. The King is ill, he is not himself. You have borne so much, bear a little more." The kind and understanding words were apparently enough to make the duchess of Kent and Strathearn (Victoria's mother) change her mind, and she and Victoria ended up staying for a short, restless night.

At any rate, the king would make up for his missteps the following year, for on Victoria's eighteenth birthday, May 24th, 1837, he bought her a piano along with several other expensive gifts. And, of course, another ball was held in her honor. But this time around, King William IV was a no-show due to poor health. It was during this engagement that Victoria was "escorted to the chair of state," where she quite literally took her place as the soon-to-be queen of Britain.

On the day that William died, it has been recalled that his loyal guards sat and waited just outside of the room where the potentate lay dying. At one point, a colonel approached them and informed them of what had happened. The stern-faced man is said to have told them, "Gentlemen—King William is dead," after which, he exclaimed, "Let us drink to the health of the Queen. God save the Queen!"

Victoria was at home in Kensington when word reached her of what had transpired. The tidings reached her mother first, and she had to wake Victoria from her bed to let her know that the lord chamberlain, the head of the royal household, wished to speak with her. Victoria, who was used to her mother always being by her side for official business, initially tried to get her mother to go with her. But her mother was forced to remind her of the burden that was so firmly affixed to her shoulders—and her shoulders only.

When she headed down the flight of stairs from her bed chambers to the room in which Lord Francis Conyngham was waiting for her, she finally threw off all of her childish habits of the past. She was now a queen. And it is said that upon becoming queen, one of the first things that Victoria did was to send off an official note to her now-widowed aunt, Adelaide, over the loss of her husband, King William.

She initially dictated for the letter to be addressed to "Her Majesty the Queen." She was then corrected by one of her attendants that the former Queen Adelaide should instead be addressed as Queen Dowager since she was now a widowed queen. But Victoria had a correction of her own, and she steadfastly replied to her handlers, "No—I wish it to be sent as it is. I am quite aware of her Majesty's altered position, but I will not be the first to remind her of it."

Chapter 4 – It's Official

"The important thing is not what they think of me, but what I think of them."

-Queen Victoria

On June 21ˢᵗ, 1837, Queen Victoria was officially declared "Queen of the United Kingdom of Great Britain and Ireland, Defender of the Faith." A large group of people was on hand to witness the queen's journey from her former home in Kensington to her new one at St. James's Palace in London. As happy as the onlookers were, however, it was noticed that the new queen did not always seem quite so joyful.

She was, at times, observed as having a rather somber countenance. Some would even go so far as to say that she seemed to be in a state of mourning. There was indeed some truth in these depictions since the new queen was—at least in some sense—mourning the loss of her old life. Like a butterfly coming out of a cocoon, she knew that her old self had to be put away in order for her new role to fully take shape.

Upon her arrival at St. James, royal musicians began to play the national anthem, and a royal salute of gunfire followed. Again, the well-wishers were there, with many cheers for the new queen resounding throughout the palace grounds. At one point, Queen

Victoria appeared at a balcony window, and overcome by the moment, the queen began to cry as she greeted her new subjects outside. She then left the balcony and returned to the matter at hand—becoming the queen of Great Britain.

Special heralds then made it official by reading out a proclamation, which ended with "God Save the Queen." The deceased King William, in the meantime, was having a funeral procession conducted in his honor where he lay in Windsor Castle. After being made queen at St. James, the queen was then whisked off to Buckingham Palace, which had only recently been constructed.

Victoria was hesitant to make this move since she was still rather fond of her previous home in Kensington. As she confided in the duke of Sussex at the time, "I do not want to go there. I love the old Kensington Gardens, where I can wander about as I please. Buckingham Palace is far too big and too grand for me." But despite these initial misgivings, Victoria knew that duty was calling her to bigger and better things.

Upon her arrival at Buckingham Palace, she was shown what would be her literal seat of power, a crimson and gold throne. After trying out the new throne for herself, she was asked by one of her attendants how she liked it, to which the new queen gleefully responded, "It's the most comfortable throne I ever sat on."

Now that she was in charge, Queen Victoria was also soon hosting her own special events. One of the most exciting of which, at least for Victoria, was when she was able to host her uncle, King Leopold I of Belgium. She was overjoyed to be able to host her beloved uncle, and it is said that she had a merry time doing so. She also held many other get-togethers in the form of dinner parties, boating events, and picnics.

But it was not all fun and games. Every morning, she would meet with her prime minister, Lord Melbourne (William Lamb, 2nd Viscount of Melbourne), to discuss the important matters of state.

With him, she discussed issues of grave importance on the world stage, as well as on the domestic front.

At the end of the day, her appointed ministers needed her signature to move their directives forward, but Victoria was not going to be a distant ruler. Early on, she proved to her advisers that she desired to be right in the thick of things. And instead of just rubber-stamping whatever British Parliament came up with, she would thoroughly look into what was being suggested. She was actually so cautious in giving her assent that on one occasion, Prime Minister Melbourne actually advised, "Your Majesty, there is no need of your examining this paper, as it is of no special importance."

Prime Minister Melbourne must have thought this particular matter to be too insignificant to worry over. But Queen Victoria, who wished to analyze every bill that passed her desk, saw things differently. She informed her prime minister, "But it is of special importance to me whether I sign a paper with which I am not thoroughly satisfied." And one can hardly blame Victoria. It would indeed be a frustrating experience for a chief executive to approve measures that they themselves were not fully informed on, only to have it come back and bite them later.

Queen Victoria wisely chose to educate herself on all legislation that was making its way to her. As a result, she was often hit with a deluge of paperwork, which took up nearly all of her time just to go through. Some of her close acquaintances at the time even began to wonder if perhaps some party members had been purposefully trying to overwhelm the queen so that she would eventually give up her hands-on approach and begin to give her automatic approval to whatever legislation they pushed forward.

If this was the case, however, they greatly underestimated the determination of Queen Victoria to stay on top of what went on in her kingdom. Aiding her in all of this was her dedicated prime minister, Lord Melbourne. Melbourne, who was many years older than the young Victoria, soon took on an almost paternalistic role with her.

The queen obviously was the more high-profile figure of the two, yet it was Prime Minister Melbourne who took the new queen under his political wings and helped to show her the ropes along the way.

They soon became remarkably close, and Victoria would later recall that she developed a kind of love for the man. Love, of course, is meant strictly in the fatherly sense of the word. In addition to Melbourne, another close adviser to Victoria at the time was a man sent by her uncle, Leopold: Baron Stockmar (Christian Friedrich). Baron Stockmar served as a trusted confidant for the queen, and Victoria knew he was a man who had the best of intentions for her.

However, Baron Stockmar also had a hidden agenda since he was doing King Leopold's bidding, specifically regarding the furthering of a potential marriage match between Leopold's nephew Albert and his niece Victoria. Leopold had kept a close watch on Prince Albert and had made sure, among other things, that he had a decent grasp of the English language. Albert, of course, who was of the maternal Coburg line, was a native German speaker. Leopold had the idea of his nephew marrying the queen of Britain, so he carefully groomed Albert for what would be expected should he become Queen Victoria's husband.

Stockmar, in the meantime, was also busily advising the queen about how important it was for her to remain non-partisan. He informed her, "The sovereign must belong to no party. Whatever party is in power has been put in power by the nation, and has a right to claim the loyalty of the Queen." Non-partisanship like this would prove much easier said than done, though. The queen was already partial to Prime Minister Melbourne and his fellow Whigs, and despite all attempts to appear non-partisan, she would be frequently perceived as being just that.

On June 28th, 1838—about one year after Victoria had become queen—her official coronation was held. Although she had been queen for around a year, the coronation could not take place until a respectable amount of time had passed since the death of the last

monarch, as a coronation is perceived as a joyous affair. And the people of England were indeed in for a grand celebration, much as was the case when Victoria was first officially declared queen. The festivities came complete with a 21-gun salute, followed by the ringing of just about every church bell within proximity, which clanged to life in the early morning hours for all to hear. And by 5 a.m., well-wishers were already flocking to Westminster Abbey.

The queen was preceded first by the carriages of important political officials, then the arrival of other royals, before, finally, Queen Victoria made her grand entrance. Upon the queen's arrival at Westminster, she was greeted by the chief officers of state. This was followed by more applause and cheers from those on the sidelines before the queen and her entourage headed back to Buckingham Palace.

The day was full of time-consuming rituals and formalities. But for Queen Victoria and her people, it was important nevertheless. The completion of these time-honored rites sealed the fate of Victoria and her kingdom once and for all. This was the final, official acknowledgment that Princess Victoria had come into her own and was indeed the queen of Great Britain.

Chapter 5 – A Honeymoon and a Bedchamber Plot

"I feel sure that no girl would go to the altar if she knew all."

-Queen Victoria

Despite all of the fanfare and goodwill of her ascension to the throne and her coronation that followed, by the year 1839, Queen Victoria had already run into some trouble. Her problems were rooted in the very partisanship that her trusted adviser Stockmar had warned her against. Although the sovereign was supposed to appear to be above the fray of partisan politics, Victoria had become partial to the Whig leader, Prime Minister Melbourne, and she found herself unable to refrain from weighing in.

She faced a real dilemma in early 1839 when vital legislation was rejected by British Parliament, forcing the current prime minister to resign. Such things are a common feature of parliamentary governments, as prime ministers can routinely be dismissed through nothing more than a simple vote of no confidence. Melbourne, seeing the writing on the wall, decided to go ahead and quit before matters reached that stage. And, so it was that Prime Minister Melbourne informed Victoria that he was vacating his position.

The queen was supposed to accept this fact, but she was so invested in Melbourne as a trusted adviser that she couldn't stand the thought of him leaving. Nevertheless, when the new prospective prime minister from the Tories—Sir Robert Peel—was invited to form a new government, she grudgingly agreed. She did, however, insist that she would still be able to keep Melbourne around as an informal adviser.

Peel was okay with this, remarking that "Lord Melbourne is too honorable a man to influence your Majesty in any way against the existing government." In other words, he figured Melbourne would be decent enough not to try and forcibly change the queen's mind about proposed legislation. The queen and her new prime minister were able to successfully compromise on this point, but Robert Peel's next demand did not go over quite so well.

With the new changes in government, he announced, "It will be desirable to make some changes in the ladies of your Majesty's household." Victoria had become quite comfortable with the women who personally attended her, and she found the idea of switching them out for fresh faces entirely intolerable. And she told Peel as much, stating, "I shall not part with any of my ladies."

Peel was apparently not expecting this stern refusal from the queen, but he insisted. "But, your Majesty, most of these ladies are closely related to the former Cabinet Ministers." Peel was reminding her that having women who were attached to dismissed Cabinet ministers in her personal employ would create a conflict of interest.

This conflict was clarified in a meeting the next day when Peel again explained to her, "There are more Whigs than Tories in the House of Commons, and if these ladies who are closely related to prominent Whigs are retained, all Europe will look upon England as the country that is governed by a party which the sovereign dislikes and in which she has no confidence."

Nevertheless, Victoria steadfastly refused to hear Peel's arguments, and soon after, she fired off a note to Melbourne, informing him of

what was happening. In this missive, the queen declared, "Do not fear, that I was not calm and composed. They wanted to deprive me of my ladies, and I suppose they would deprive me next of my dressers and housemaids; they wished to treat me like a girl, but I will show them that I am Queen of England."

Although Queen Victoria felt that she was making an important stand as the sovereign of Great Britain, Melbourne wasn't all that impressed. In many ways, Victoria's stance appeared to be an outrageously selfish one. She steadfastly stood up to the designs of the new prime minister but not because she objected to any piece of policy or legislation. Rather, she stood up to him simply out of a desire to avoid the discomfort of having to hire new personal attendants.

Victoria, though, must have been proud of herself for standing her ground, but to others, it more than likely came off as an incredibly petty and unnecessary act (if not an outright abuse) of power. Melbourne and his fellow party members themselves were deeply concerned over the drama that had erupted, and they quickly sought out some sort of compromise that would appease both Peel and the queen.

It was suggested that perhaps the queen could be convinced to part with at least the most partisan of her ladies. But before any such attempt of appeasement could be made, Peel took the initiative himself and refused to become the prime minister. This meant that a potential Cabinet of Tories was no longer in the works, and Melbourne was eventually convinced to stay on as the prime minister and lead the government.

This infamous debacle would go down in history as the Bedchamber Plot or the Bedchamber Crisis. As you might have guessed, this event was named such because this colossal reversal of parliamentary affairs was rooted in the fact that the queen simply did not wish to have to hire new help for her bedchamber. Or, as the resigned Peel explained it, "The Prime Minister is responsible for the

acts of the Queen, and it is a large matter if she refuses to follow his advice when he believes that the good of the realm demands a certain course. She is not the Queen of the whole country, she is only the Queen of the Whigs, and the whole thing is a plot to keep the Whigs in power."

This sentiment was even more bluntly put by some of his fellow Tories when it was declared that they "stand by the constitution of Great Britain, not by the whims of a girl of nineteen." Yes, it certainly didn't look good for the nineteen-year-old queen to create paralysis in British governance merely because she didn't want to part with her favorite chambermaids. But, for the sake of giving Victoria's motives the benefit of the doubt, she was in a fairly difficult position at the time.

After all, she was a young queen who was fearful of becoming increasingly isolated. She had become close to certain attendants and did not wish to lose the closeness that had just begun to emerge. For her, she was simply trying to hang on to some semblance of continuity since the ground beneath her feet often felt unstable. At any rate, it was due to this controversy that Victoria's once soaring popularity began to plummet just one year into her reign.

The situation was indeed distressing, and soon, the chaos that had unfolded reached the attention of Victoria's uncle, King Leopold I of Belgium. Leopold, wishing to help ease some of the isolation that Victoria was feeling, had Prince Albert come to pay her a visit. Leopold had more on his mind than just having Albert engage in a friendly chat with Victoria, though. He was looking to have the two marry each other.

And so, in the fall of 1839, he sent Albert, who was accompanied by his brother Ernest, to provide company to the queen. Victoria knew exactly what the intent of the visit was, and she found herself preparing to propose to Albert. Yes, even though back then (and largely to this day) it was incumbent upon the male marriage prospect to propose, it was expected for Victoria to be the one to suggest

marriage to her potential partner or, as it would be referred to in royal terms, her consort since she was a queen,.

And this was apparently what she did. Her accepting fiancé later described the event in great detail to his grandmother. As he recalled, "The Queen sent for me alone to her room the other day, and declared to me in a genuine outburst of affection that I have gained her whole heart, and would make her intensely happy if I would make her the sacrifice of sharing her life with her, for she said she looked upon it as a sacrifice. The only thing that troubled her was that she did not think she was worthy of me."

It must have been a touching scene to see this great monarch showing such vulnerability in expressing her feelings for Albert. Fortunately for her, Albert was more than willing to take on the "sacrifice" of which she spoke, and the couple was promptly engaged to be married.

Queen Victoria had expressed her concern over the sacrifices that she knew that Albert would have to make as her husband. She knew that the husband of a queen would always be overshadowed by their spouse, and she also knew that since he was of German background, he would most likely be perceived as an interloper, despite his best efforts to be well liked and to fit in. Indeed, she knew this all too well with the painful experiences of her mother, who was often viewed as an outsider.

As it turns out, however, many of her fears proved to be overblown. Albert, who was quite an amiable and talented man, would eventually win over the hearts of the British, who would accept him as one of their own.

In November of 1839, Victoria convened a council to let her intentions be officially known. She proclaimed to those in attendance, "I have caused you to be summoned at the present time in order that I may acquaint you with my resolution in a matter which deeply concerns the welfare of my people and the happiness of my future

life. It is my intention to ally myself in marriage with Prince Albert of Saxe Coburg and Gotha. Deeply impressed with the solemnity of the engagement which I am about to contract I have not come to this decision without mature consideration, nor without feeling a strong assurance that, with the blessing of Almighty God, it will at once secure my domestic felicity and serve the interests of my country. I have thought fit to make known this resolution to you at this early period in order that you may be apprised of a matter so highly important to me and to my kingdom, and which I persuade myself will be most acceptable to all my loving subjects."

Soon after this private proclamation, on January 16th, 1840, the queen publicly affirmed her intentions by declaring right in front of British Parliament that she and Albert had become engaged to be married. The marriage itself would take place on February 10th, 1840.

Not everyone was happy with these tidings. The previously spurned Tories, in particular, began to openly speculate about the queen's prospective husband. Predictably enough, some latched onto his foreign origins and began to suggest that perhaps Albert was a fanatic Catholic who would not be loyal to Protestant-leaning Great Britain. Nevertheless, despite all the talk of the court gossips, the couple did indeed get married as planned. The honeymoon was a short one, however, as it was rushed along in just a few days.

Albert had actually tried to get Victoria to take more time off, but the queen quickly reminded him of the "sacrifice" one had to make when dealing with a monarch. She told her new husband, "You forget, my dearest Love, that I am the Sovereign, and that business can't stop and wait for nothing." Nevertheless, Victoria would recall one of those few nights allotted for their honeymoon with fond reverence.

She later remarked, "His [Albert's] excessive love and affection gave me feelings of heavenly love and happiness I never could have hoped to have felt before! Really—how can I ever be thankful enough to have such a husband!" And she ended her account of their first

outing as husband and wife with the words, "This was the happiest day of my life!"

Albert, for his part, however, would soon learn how minimal his role would really be. He would become a hanger-on in the palace without too much to do. He was also largely kept in the dark about matters of state. The only information he could discern was the generalities derived by the queen's mood. If she seemed to have taken on a particularly dark mood, he knew that all was not well in her world of statecraft.

It was not Albert's role to advise her on what to do, though; rather, his role involved lifting her spirits. And he was often there to get her out of any negative malaise in which she might become stuck. Albert voiced some of these feelings of helplessness as the queen's spouse in a missive he sent to his friend, Prince Wilhelm (William) of Löwenstein. He complained to Prince Wilhelm that he often felt that "he was not the master but only the husband in the house."

Due to his lower status in comparison to his wife, Queen Victoria, Prince Albert felt insecure as a husband. Others also tried to provoke insecurity in the prince, with some even going as far as to slander his ability to procreate. A certain duchess of Bedford, apparently, even began a rumor that Prince Albert was somehow impotent. However, this was dispelled when it was soon determined that the queen was pregnant with Albert's child.

Chapter 6 – The Many Labors of a Queen

"Great events make me quiet and calm; it is only trifles that irritate my nerves."

-Queen Victoria

After marrying Prince Albert, Victoria was pleased to see just how supportive of a husband that her Prince Charming really was. And Albert, even though he was unable to affect national policy, turned out to be an excellent manager of the palace's domestic life. This oversight was sorely needed since much in the way of how the palace was run was in complete disarray.

Security was also too lax. It was so bad, in fact, that at one point, a young man was actually discovered to have been squatting in one of the rooms of the palace. The man had not broken in; rather, he simply entered through unlocked gates and had walked right past the men who were supposed to guard against intruders. It seems that there was simply no accountability among the guards, and if they wanted to step away from their posts for any reason, they did. It was most likely during one of these fits of dereliction that the intruder slipped into the palace unnoticed. They say a man's house is his

castle, and you would think that the palace of Prince Albert and Queen Victoria would at least be as impregnable as one. But it was not. It was out of concern for order, safety, and security that Prince Albert brought all of these matters up with the prime minister.

These matters of securing the palace became even more important after it was learned that the queen was pregnant. The matter was also brought up as to what would happen if the queen abruptly perished after giving birth to her child. Such matters were important to discuss during those days since it was rather common for women to die in childbirth. Even more troubling, however, was the threat of assassination.

The threat of bodily harm was indeed real. On June 10th, 1840, in fact, shortly after the prince and the queen were married, an attempt was made on Queen Victoria's life. A troubled man had apparently come across the queen and the prince's carriage at random, and he opened fire. He shot at the queen twice, but fortunately for her, this would-be assassin had bad aim. He managed to miss both times.

The shooter was tackled by enraged onlookers and hauled off to a nearby police station. The shooter was a man named Edward Oxford, and he had previously worked in a bar before taking up arms against Britain's sovereign. No clear reason as to why he committed the act has ever been given, other than the fact that he was mentally imbalanced.

And although he was found guilty of attempted murder, it was deemed that he was insane at the time. Edward was then shuffled off to an insane asylum, where he would remain for the next thirty-five years. After this, he was allowed to move to the British territory of Australia, where he essentially lived out the rest of his days as an exile.

Due to threats of violence such as the one illustrated above, it was determined ahead of time that Albert himself would become regent until the child was old enough to reign on their own. The queen ended up giving birth to a healthy baby girl on November 21st, 1840.

This baby would be named Victoria in honor of her mother. But in order to differentiate between the two, she would ultimately go by the name of Vicky.

The nation was excited at the prospect of the birth of a new royal, but Victoria was a little less than enthused. She always despised the whole process of childbirth, and she actually thought that babies were kind of ugly. In fact, she was known to remark that they looked to her a little bit like frogs.

Nevertheless, the political intrigue of the realm didn't give her much time to contemplate such matters. In the following year, 1841, the Queen's preferred prime minister, Lord Melbourne, and the Whig Party were once again bested by Robert Peel and the Tories. The Tories were now determined to tackle reforming the flagging British economy and various other domestic problems. Particularly popular was proposed legislation to increase the prosperity of working-class Britons.

In this vein, a sudden flurry of bills focused on improving everything from dangerous work environments to proper childhood education was put forward, and this time around, they weren't going to be thwarted by Victoria's desires to keep the same familiar attendants in her bedchamber. The queen, at any rate, was a little too preoccupied at this point to run much interference.

After all, she was a married woman with a baby, and she soon had another one on the way. Furthermore, with her husband, Prince Albert, acting as her most trusted adviser rather than any party-affiliated prime minister, she was secure enough to allow the political fortunes of Parliament to shift as they may.

Victoria, in the meantime, gave birth to her next child, a healthy baby boy, on November 9th, 1841. The child was named Albert Edward in honor of his father. It was a joyous occasion for the royal family to have a direct male heir. The queen herself commemorated

the event by decreeing that all prisoners who had behaved well should have their punishment reduced.

Needless to say, this baby boy was born with some pretty big expectations. And by the time the prince reached his first month of life, he had already been dubbed the prince of Wales and the earl of Chester.

The happiness of the royal family would be disturbed in 1842, however, when the queen once again faced an assassination attempt. The assassin—John Francis—had ambushed the queen's carriage as he passed Constitution Hill. Fortunately, though, just as was the case before, the gunman missed his mark.

In order to reassure the public that she was fine, the queen actually attended an opera concert in full view shortly thereafter. But the danger was far from over. Another attempt was made a short time later when a would-be assassin once again tried to shoot into the queen's carriage. This time, however, the bullet failed to even discharge, and the assailant was immediately taken into custody.

This domestic disturbance would pale in comparison when it came to the international turmoil that had begun to erupt in late 1841. Around this time, the British outposts in Afghanistan had been rocked by a massive uprising of local Afghans. Yes, in a land that has been commonly referred to as the "graveyard of empires," all hell was about to break loose. On November 2nd of that year, rebels sprouted up in the city of Kabul and threatened the British forces in the region.

The elderly general in charge of British operations—John Elphinstone—seemed to flinch during the onslaught and ordered a hastily convened withdrawal. This led to a grand exodus of British people and possessions in the bitterly cold first week of January. Beset by the cold, rough terrain, and an unrelenting enemy, the whole lot of them were eventually butchered or taken captive, save for one sole survivor—one Dr. William Brydon, who managed to reach the British enclave in Jellalabad.

Sir Robert Sale, in the meantime, was on the march with his troops when he heard word of what had happened. He and his men ended up encountering the same rebels, but they were able to beat them well enough to get to the stronghold of Jellalabad. Here, the outnumbered British troops sought to make a desperate stand against their attackers. They ended up being holed up for about five months before Sale sent his soldiers on the offensive against their attackers.

The offensive was a success and managed to catch the Afghan rebels off guard. British troops then marched on Kabul and put down any remaining resistance. And to teach the Afghans a lesson, the British even went as far as to raze the great bazaar so that all could understand that anyone who opposed British rule would go up in flames.

While all of this was going on, further conflicts were erupting in British possessions in China. Yes, the city we know today as Hong Kong was once a British colony right on mainland China. In fact, Britain would go on to control Hong Kong all the way until 1997. Upon returning Hong Kong to China, the British had the Chinese agree to allow for the so-called "one country, two Systems" rule. This means that although China can lay claim to Hong Kong, it will not try to interfere with the system of governance already at work in the region.

It is for this reason that Hong Kong is so at odds with mainland China today. China is an authoritarian communist country, whereas Hong Kong is a capitalist, free market, democratic enclave. In what amounts to one of the greatest flashpoints of modern times, the citizens of modern Hong Kong would very much like to remain a bastion of democracy, yet China seeks to slowly reshape Hong Kong into something more palatable for the communist regime.

If you asked your average resident of Hong Kong today if they would prefer to go back to being a British colonist rather than being absorbed into China, an astonishing number would say yes! The fact

is that most in Hong Kong would rather be under British rule than Chinese authoritarianism.

In 1841, however, few knew just how history would unfold for this far-flung region in the Far East. For a few years, the British had been conducting a heavy-handed trade policy with China and had become incensed when China refused to abide by treaties that had been ratified. This led to bouts of so-called "gunboat diplomacy," in which the British tried to get China to live up to its agreements by force.

Likewise, many ports were forcibly opened up to trade, including Hong Kong, which ultimately came under British control in 1841. The following year, the British were at war once again when skirmishes erupted in colonial India. The local population, partially inspired by the Afghan rebellion, began an uprising of their own against the British. The task of putting out this fire was given to General Sir Charles Napier.

It is said that under fire from the rebels, Napier had his soldiers conduct a daring charge right into their opponents. This led to gruesome close-range combat. A terrible back-and-forth struggle ensued, but in the end, the British Army came out on top.

With her empire struggling to maintain its hold on various portions of the globe, Victoria, in the meantime, would claim some new ground of her own.

Chapter 7 – Domestic Squabbles and Power Struggles

"A marriage is no amusement but a solemn act, and generally a sad one."

-Queen Victoria

In January of 1842, Victoria and her husband Albert decided to take a break from the drama and intrigue of London by vacationing in Claremont, a mansion near Surrey, England. The trip was cut short, however, when they received word that their daughter Vicky had become ill. They came home to find the little girl "pale and thin" It was a distressing sight, and as often happens when parents face such challenging situations, Victoria and Albert began to point fingers and ultimately blamed each other.

At one point, Albert seemed to put much of the blame on Queen Victoria's shoulders, claiming that her mismanagement of their child's care was tantamount to neglect. He also blamed Victoria's old trusted attendant, Louise Lehzen, and basically accused them both of nearly killing little Vicky. Victoria, of course, wasn't about to take such accusations too kindly, and she immediately began to unload on what was otherwise her usual loving husband.

She shot back that Albert was just jealous of her relationship with Lehzen and then went on to say that she was sorry she had ever married him. It's certainly a stunning thing to tell your spouse, but it most certainly wasn't the first time a wife said such a thing to her husband. In the heat of an argument, spouses often say things they come to regret. And Victoria did indeed regret her remarks, later admitting that when she was angry, she tended to say hurtful things that she didn't really mean.

As she herself later put it, "There is often an irritability in me which (like Sunday last which began the whole misery) makes me say cross and odious things which I don't believe myself and which I fear hurt A. [Albert], but which he should not believe, but I will strive to conquer it though I knew before I married that this would be a trouble; I therefore wished not to marry, as the two years and a half, when I was so completely my own mistress made it difficult for me to control myself and to bend to another's will, but I trust I shall be able to conquer it."

She claimed it was just a way that she lashed out but that she didn't really mean the things that she said. Albert, however, took the harsh words pretty hard. And after he stormed out, he fired off a letter to her shortly thereafter that laid out his wounded feelings and his still forming accusations very plainly. Albert charged, "Doctor Clark has mismanaged the child and poisoned her with calomel and you have starved her. I shall have nothing more to do with it; take the child away and do as you like and if she dies you will have it on your conscience."

Queen Victoria, who was in deep distress, sought out the help of her old adviser Baron Stockmar for help. But when Albert was approached by Stockmar, he doubled down on his complaints and retrained his focus on Lehzen. In his fury, he unabashedly told Stockmar, "Lehzen is a crazy, common, stupid intriguer, obsessed with lust of power, who regards herself as a demi-god, and anyone who refuses to acknowledge her as such is a criminal."

He then softened his outlook on his own wife, stating, "I on the other hand regard Victoria as naturally a fine character but warped in many respects by wrong upbringing." As Albert and Victoria continued to use Stockmar as their go-between, Victoria informed the baron that she "forgave Albert's thoughtless words."

However, Albert was not ready to backtrack; instead, he doubled down. Upon hearing Victoria's response, he proclaimed, "All the disagreeableness I suffer comes from one and the same person and that is precisely the person whom Victoria chooses for her friend and confidante. Victoria is too hasty and passionate for me to be able often to speak of my difficulties. She will not hear me out but flies into a rage and overwhelms me with reproaches and suspiciousness, want of trust, ambition, envy etcetera...There are, therefore, two ways open to me: (1) to keep silence and go away (in which case I am like a schoolboy who has had a dressing-down from his mother and goes off snubbed), (2) I can be still more violent (and then we have scenes...which I hate because I am so sorry for Victoria in her misery)."

It was a major power struggle between two people very close to the queen. Albert had clashed with Lehzen ever since he had married Victoria, and now it seems that he found the perfect opportunity to displace her. He was basically telling Victoria that it was either him or Lehzen—she had to decide. Victoria, of course, chose her husband. In the end, she only insisted that Lehzen be given a nice, quiet home to reward her for her past services. To this last point, Albert gave his consent.

So, on July 25th, 1842, the ax fell on Lehzen, and Albert terminated her services. She was then sent packing to Germany. Stockmar, in the meantime, did his best to convince Victoria that it was the best thing for all involved. After recalling her last visit, Victoria reported, "I went to see my dear good Lehzen and found her very cheerful, saying she felt it was necessary for her health to go away, for of course, I did not require her so much now, and would find others to help me, whilst

she could still help me in doing little things for me abroad. She repeated, she would be ready to come to me, whenever I wanted, so that I can see her from time to time. Altogether, nothing could have been more satisfactory and pleasant than was our little interview. Walked out in the afternoon with Albert, and when we came home, we played on the piano."

Despite their previous affection, in the end, Victoria didn't even get to say goodbye, as Lehzen left without bothering to exchange pleasantries with the queen. Lehzen later explained that she did this to avoid hurt feelings. As Victoria would later recall, "I had a letter from my dear Lehzen in which she took leave of me in writing, thinking it would be less painful than seeing me and as the wind had abated, and everything was ready for her departure, she had started off at once. This naturally upset me, and I so regret not being able to embrace her once more, though on the other hand I am much relieved at being spared the painful parting."

Nevertheless, despite this attempt at shielding her feelings, Victoria went on to say, "But I felt it very much. Though I had, in fact, seen but little of my dear good Lehzen since our marriage, still the thought that she was far away now, and all alone, made me very sad. I can never forget that she was for many years everything to me and I shall be forever grateful and devotedly attached to her. Still for herself and for all, she has done the wisest thing."

The new home that Lehzen ended up taking was one with her own sister over in the town of Bückeburg, close to Hanover, Germany. She was also given a lifelong pension, which would amount to about $104,000 in today's US dollars. And to top it all off, Victoria gifted her an expensive carriage so that she would be sure to have the best in 19th-century transportation. Yes, despite all of Prince Albert's rancor, Lehzen was bought off quite handsomely.

Nevertheless, with Lehzen gone, Albert could consider himself the master of his domain. He began to micromanage just about every aspect of domestic life at the palace. He also kept a close watch on

Queen Victoria's finances. By all accounts, it seems that this was not exactly something that Victoria opposed; in fact, she seemed to have encouraged it. Since Albert was essentially taking over all the micromanaging that attendants like Lehzen had carried out for much of Victoria's life, the queen allowed him to have free rein in the home.

This was not appreciated by Victoria's other family members, however, who seemed to perceive him to be an upstart of sorts. Nevertheless, Albert continued to try and throw his weight around. Along with running the show at home, he also joined up with several civic organizations that were focused on aiding the poor and improving life for the general populace in the British Empire. These groups had lofty names, such as the Society for Improving the Condition of the Labouring Classes and the Society for the Extinction of the Slave Trade and for the Civilization of Africa.

Still, Victoria knew that her husband wanted to have more of an impact, and in June of 1842, she sought the ear of Prime Minister Robert Peel to see if she could somehow help him. She explained to Peel that her "dear Albert" was in an awfully "awkward and painful position." In order to improve this supposedly awkward state, she asked Peel if Albert could receive a bit of an upgrade to his official title. She wanted him to be known as the king consort, just as the queen of a natural-born king might be known as the queen consort.

Tradition was against this, however, but Victoria made it clear that she didn't like it. She stated, "It seemed to me very wrong that the reigning Queen's husband should not have the same." In other words, she figured that instead of being stuck for all eternity as a prince, Albert should be named king consort.

But, as the queen herself later explained, "Sir Robert Peel thought the reason was a fear that a Prince Consort might usurp the Queen's right. This I cannot agree in, but Sir Robert expressed his readiness and anxiety to do what he could, while deprecating a long discussion in Parliament, which might not make Albert's position more agreeable. I remarked that the position of a Prince Consort must be

painful and humiliating to any man and that at times I almost felt it would have been fairer to him, for me not to have married him. But he was so good and kind and had loved me for myself." Victoria would continue throughout the years to try and get Albert named king consort, but her efforts would ultimately fall flat.

Chapter 8 – Playing with a House of Cards

"We are not interested in the possibilities of defeat. They do not exist."

-Queen Victoria

The year 1843 brought more changes for Victoria's family, for that year she gave birth to another daughter: Alice. Little Alice was born on April 25th, 1843. Her full name was Alice Maud Mary, but she acquired the nickname of Fatima. The reason? Because she was fat! This baby was apparently quite healthy, and she was born with a little more weight than most.

Queen Victoria, for her part, was just happy that the ordeal was over. As she put it, "At 5 minutes past 4, a fine, healthy girl was born and all my sufferings had come to an end!" Another thing that Victoria appreciated was the fact that Albert had ended the practice of having several dozen men of state waiting outside to confirm the birth of a new royal.

Thankful for the newfound privacy, Victoria later recalled, "I felt extremely quiet and comfortable afterwards and slept a good deal. My beloved Albert, who had watched so tenderly over me the whole time

had many people to see, and such numbers of letters to write." She and Albert, for once, had a chance to relax. They read to each other and talked, and when Victoria was up for it, they went out for walks in the palace garden.

After sufficiently recovering from giving birth to Alice, Victoria prepared for a state trip abroad to France. English and French relations had seesawed throughout the centuries, and proper maintenance with Great Britain's neighbor across the English Channel was always important. Victoria left for France on her own personal yacht on September 1st, 1843. Upon her arrival in France, she was met by the French king and queen. They were then given a guided tour of the Château d' EU, the site where William the Conqueror wed his wife. This was meant to shore up the shared ties that bound French and English history together.

Queen Victoria was then treated to a review of the French soldiers. In all, the queen ended up staying until September 7th before heading back across the English Channel. Shortly after her return, her family would be rocked by an unexpected sadness. In January of 1844, Albert's father passed away. It was a hard blow for Albert to deal with, but the love of his wife helped to pull him through it.

In fact, he referred to Victoria as nothing short of being his "consoling angel." At one point, he even stated to Stockmar, "She is the treasure on which my whole existence rests." After dealing with the near-break-up of the pair, Stockmar must have at least been pleased of the apparently solid bond that emerged through this tragic loss. This mourning process was apparently only interrupted when a matter of much less seriousness came to the royal couple's attention.

They were visited by Charles Sherwood Stratton, the circus performer otherwise known as General Tom Thumb. Stratton was born with a condition that limited his height. He would only grow to be a little over three feet tall. At the time of his visit to Queen Victoria, he was in the employ of the infamous P. T. Barnum, touring far and wide to dance, mimic famous figures such as Napoleon, and otherwise

make people laugh. And Victoria and company, despite their recent melancholy, did find it within themselves to laugh at what they were seeing and hearing.

However, Victoria began to develop some measure of pity for Stratton himself. As she would later reflect, "One cannot help feeling very sorry for the poor little thing and wishing he could be properly cared for, for the people who show him off tease him a good deal, I should think." Victoria was most likely right in her estimation of events, as Stratton's condition most certainly was being exploited. Then again, Stratton would later go on to become filthy rich. So rich, in fact, that he would one day bail P. T. Barnum himself out when the ringmaster fell on hard economic times. And it was all thanks to having the opportunity he was given to travel the world as a performer. An opportunity given to him by P. T. Barnum and all the other circus handlers who exploited him. At any rate, Victoria and company enjoyed the show that Stratton put on and were sure to send plenty of money and gifts to show their gratitude.

Around this time, Victoria became pregnant once again. It was a pregnancy that would lead to the birth of her second son: Alfred Ernest Albert. Alfred was born on August 6th, 1844. She gave a frank description of the child's appearance, writing shortly after his birth, "The baby has a quantity of long dark hair, which none of the others had, large blue eyes and a large nose."

Prince Albert, in the meantime, was busy upgrading Buckingham Palace for his growing family. He also took it upon himself to greatly revamp the trappings of Windsor Castle, adding, among other things, "a farm, a dairy and kennels." But perhaps the most pivotal home improvement venture that Albert embarked upon was the overseeing of the construction of a vacation home on the Isle of Wight, which would become known as the Osborne House.

The Isle of Wight was a place that was dear to Victoria's heart since she had vacationed there previously in her youth. Albert knew as much, and he used his allotted allowance as a prince to purchase the

land himself. He then busied himself with all aspects of the home's construction, making sure that everything was perfect. The initial rendering, however, was considered too small in light of Albert and Victoria's ever-increasing brood of children, so it was determined that the Osborne House must be enlarged.

This was done through the help of "master builder" Thomas Cubitt. The enlargement was indeed wise because, predictably enough, Victoria was soon pregnant once again. Her latest child—Helena Augusta Victoria—was born on May 25th, 1846.

Just prior to Helena's birth, the queen was faced with tremendous domestic turmoil. For it was in the spring of 1846 that much of Ireland was rocked with the so-called potato famine.

The potato had been a staple of the Irish diet. The crop was severely disrupted, however, by an outbreak of potato blight, which caused widespread crop failure. Deprived of a mainstay of their diet, the Irish began to seriously suffer, and the severe conditions in Ireland provoked uprisings and rebellions.

Whig Prime Minister Robert Peel initially tried his best to help the Irish. He even went as far as to set up a clandestine operation to buy corn from America with which to feed the starving masses. It had to be secretive since British and American relations were not at their best in the 1840s. These efforts ultimately fell flat, however, with late shipments and local difficulties in processing and distributing the corn.

Growing increasingly agitated, the Irish began to take to the streets in protest. Peel took a hard line against this by trying to pass his so-called Irish Coercion Bill. However, this legislation was highly opposed by the Tories, and it ultimately failed to gain muster in Parliament. This meant that Peel was suddenly the odd man out, so he resigned as prime minister. Robert Peel showed up at Osborne House himself to inform Queen Victoria as to what was transpiring. Victoria would later make mention of this moment in her diary. She wrote, "His loss is an immense one, to us, to the Country, and to all

Europe and I tremble for the future, and for the consequences it may bring."

The consequences were indeed dire, as several thousand Irish perished from the lack of food, and many more immigrated to the United States in order to escape the crisis. Victoria, in the meantime, was so enthused about her new baby girl and happy family life in Osborne House at the Isle of Wight that she seemed to tune much of it out.

This can be seen when she noted, "Really when one is so happy and blessed in one's home life, as I am, Politics must take only a 2nd place." Of course, all of the Irish dying of starvation certainly wouldn't have taken too kindly to the fact that the Queen was so easily able to ignore their plight and make their suffering "2nd place" in her mind while she focused on her "home life."

With Tory Robert Peel now removed from the government, the queen was presented with another Whig prime minister—Lord John Russell. It was on Russel's shoulders to ease the suffering of Ireland, as well as to manage impending developments farther abroad.

Victoria, in the meantime, had once again become pregnant. This latest pregnancy would lead to the birth of Louise Caroline Alberta on March 18th, 1848. The couple would not have much time to enjoy their new daughter, though.

Due to impending developments, Queen Victoria was forced to spend much of her days pouring over dispatches from Europe as well as places farther abroad. The telegraph may have been in its infancy, but there was more than enough material for it to broadcast across its wires. There were uprisings, unrests, rebellions, and, yes, rumors of war in much abundance.

Many of the conflicts that erupted in 1848 were due to failures of the old political status quo. Many parts of the world found the more or less "feudal" systems that ruled over them ineffective and they had begun to rail against them. Even though the constitutional monarchy

did make efforts to curtail its effect, the potato famine in Ireland ran along similar lines.

Although the prime minister dealt with the vast bulk of day-to-day affairs, the queen and her prince consort did indeed feel pressured to stay abreast of what was happening around them. Particularly of interest were the revolutions occurring in Europe. France had just undergone its so-called February Revolution, throwing King Louis Philippe off the throne and ushing in the Second Republic.

Also, revolutionary movements in Italian, Austrian, and German regions (*regions* must be stressed since many of the principalities that make up these nations today were not part of a united nation state at the time) increasingly kept them on notice. These tidings filled Victoria with doubt, so much so that she was prompted to make a diary entry in which she stated, "Uncertainty everywhere, as well as for the future of our children, unarmed me, and I quite gave way to my grief. I feel grown 20 years older, and as if I could not anymore think of any amusement. I tremble at the thought of what may possibly await us here."

It was indeed hard to fathom what all of these revolutionary activities would bring about. Victoria, for example, could not possibly have foreseen that the revolutions rocking Italian and German domains would lead to the birth of their modern nation state counterparts. Nor could she have seen the eventual dissolution of the Hapsburg dynasty or, for that matter, the Russian monarchy. But it could be said that the seeds for all of these things were planted all the way back in that fateful year of 1848.

Simply put, many were actively rethinking the old ways of doing things and looking to throw off what they perceived to be the yoke of the past. Victoria herself, of course, was tied to the ancient tradition of monarchy, and she couldn't help but feel a bit insecure in the knowledge that much of the world was eagerly attempting to dispense with their respective ties to the regime.

As it pertains to France, in particular, Britain actually played an active role in evacuating King Louis Philippe, and his wife, Maria Amalia, out of France. They were whisked out of the country when things got too dangerous for them to stay any longer. The situation had been so dire that they literally left with nothing more than the clothing on their backs when they arrived at Buckingham Palace.

Their grown daughter Clémentine and her spouse, August of Saxe-Coburg and Gotha, came along with them. Clémentine, who was close in age to Victoria herself, filled the British queen in on all of the horrid details of their escape. Victoria noted all of this in her journal at the time, writing, "What could be more dreadful. Poor Clem says she can't get to sleep, constantly seeing before her those horrible faces, and hearing these dreadful cries and shrieks. Then she said how melancholy were the thoughts of the future which God knows they are, if one tries to imagine the situation of the poor Royal Family. One can hardly grasp the desolation and misery of their most undeserved position."

And by April, with the Chartist uprising in the works, Queen Victoria and her family began to fear that this rebellious streak would take root much closer to home. The Chartists, who were basically grassroots, British working-class reformers, dated back to the so-called People's Charter of 1838, which highlighted several reforms demanded by the working class.

The movement ebbed and flowed over the years, but by the spring of 1848, it had really picked up momentum. And in April of that year, it was rumored that a mob of Chartists were going to march on London. Fearing the worst, Victoria and her family were evacuated from the city on April 10th in order to hole up in the higher ground of the Osborne House.

Victoria captured her distress at the time by writing, "The sorrow at the state of Germany, at the distress and ruin all round, added to very bad news from Ireland, and alarm in people's minds at the great

meeting which is to take place in London on the 10th, are trying my poor Albert very much."

As it turned out, the fears of a Chartist revolution were overblown. The organizers had hoped to have hundreds of thousands of demonstrators marching through London's streets. In the end, their numbers were more around twenty-five thousand people. Even so, a cavalry and infantry of some 10,000 soldiers, as well as an auxiliary force of 100,000 citizen volunteers, were put in place just in case things were to get out of control. The rainy weather also proved helpful since it seemed to literally rain on the Chartists' parade.

As such, the speakers tasked with exciting the gathered crowd became dispirited, and they were entirely unable to inspire anyone to do much of anything, let alone overthrow the British government. In the end, those assembled dispersed in peaceful (if not entirely despondent) fashion.

The homegrown threat to Victoria's rule appeared to be over, yet just shortly after their return home, Albert himself was personally threatened. They were on their way back from the opera house one evening when a deranged individual jogged up to their horse-drawn carriage and shouted at Prince Albert. According to Victoria's later recollection, "A man ran up to the carriage on Albert's side, where the window was open, saying several times over something like 'a real murderer.' This frightened me dreadfully, on account of the Chartist troubles and I could not get over it for some time."

During all of this drama and intrigue, Victoria's youngest daughter, Louise, was growing. The baby seemed to be the one bright spot in Victoria's life during this troubling period. And by the time the child was a year old, Victoria beamed, "May God bless the dear little child, who is so fat, strong, and well again. She was born in the most eventful times, and ought to be something peculiar in consequence."

Victoria would get pregnant again shortly thereafter and give birth to yet another son, Arthur, who was born on May 1st, 1850. Victoria loved her son, and she showered him with unabashed favoritism. At one point, she actually remarked that he "was dearer than the rest put together."

Prince Consort Albert and Queen Victoria managed to become split on how they should deal with the political turmoil of the day. Albert, who had taken it upon himself to be involved with charitable organizations, was somewhat in favor of reform, whereas it was the queen's instinct to crush dissent when it emerged. Queen Victoria was of the view that if you give an inch, you give a mile. She believed that one had to be strong against one's opposition; otherwise, they would be inspired to become even more demanding and take advantage.

She may not have been that far from the truth, considering what would happen to some of her royal peers. In 1918, just a couple of decades after Queen Victoria's eventual demise in 1901, the whole Russian royal family was slaughtered by communist insurgents after giving in to demands for reform.

Victoria feared much the same. She thought that she had to be strong in order to survive. Sometimes it seemed as if she was playing with a house of cards, being extremely careful with how each policy was placed. But this was because she instinctively believed that giving in to too many demands too quickly just might bring the monarchy down entirely.

Chapter 9 – Hard Choices to Make

"Give my people plenty of beer, good beer, and cheap beer, and you will have no revolution among them."

-Queen Victoria

As the year 1849 came to a close, Victoria was saddened to learn of Queen Dowager Adelaide's passing on December 2nd, 1849. And the new year of 1850 wasn't much better since it, too, would be full of instances in which those close to Victoria and her husband abruptly passed away. On top of losing her aunt, Victoria also lost Sir Robert Peel, who would die in a freak accident after being tossed from his steed. The duke of Cambridge—Victoria's uncle—would pass away that year as well. Victoria's uncle, Leopold, would lose his wife, Louise of Orléans. The French-king-turned-refugee Louis Philippe perished before the year was out as well.

Even more distressing, however, was an incident that occurred to Queen Victoria that threatened her own personal safety. She was used to death threats and even assassins attempting to take potshots at her. But on this distressful occasion, the hatred of others became even more personal. She was seated in her carriage, being driven back to

the palace, when the carriage was greeted by a crowd of well-wishers. It was quite customary for the carriage to slow down or even come to a stop so that Victoria could greet them.

Most were happy to see her, but one man had ill intent in mind. This stranger walked right up to the side of the carriage and proceeded to strike Victoria across the face with his walking stick. It is indeed shocking even now to consider it, but yes, it really happened—Victoria, the Queen of Great Britain, was whacked upside the head with some random man's cane.

As Victoria herself would later recall of the incident, "I felt myself violently thrown by a blow to the left of the carriage. My impulse had been to throw myself that way, not knowing what was coming next. My bonnet was crushed, and on putting my hand up to my forehead, I felt an immense bruise on the right side, fortunately well above the temple and eyes! The man was instantly caught by the collar, and then I got up in the carriage, having quite recovered myself, and telling the good people who anxiously surrounded me, 'I am not hurt,' I saw him violently pulled about by the people. Poor Fanny was so overcome, that she began to cry."

Once again, however, even in the midst of all these troubling developments, Victoria and her husband Albert found a silver lining through the birth of a new child. On May 1ˢᵗ, 1850, their son Arthur William Patrick Albert was born. Although Arthur was far too distant in birth order to ever hope to ascend the British throne, he would one day become a respected figure in the British Empire. Among other things, he would serve with distinction as the governor general of Canada.

The following year, Victoria's husband, Prince Albert, really proved his mettle by putting together a grand exhibit called the Great Exhibition of Work. This grand affair would be one of the prince's crowning achievements in its forward-thinking display of how the world of work can be refined to better benefit humanity. It is said that these efforts were made in order to speak directly to the working

classes, most especially the Chartists, of possible plans to better their lives.

The exhibit did much more than that since it also showcased all the latest in technological development. It was in many ways a precursor to the World's Fairs that would come to celebrate progress in America. Queen Victoria, for her part, was absolutely beaming over her husband's efforts, and her journal entries of the time document her enthusiasm. She wrote, "Albert's dearest name is immortalized with this great conception. It was the happiest, proudest day of my life and I can think of nothing else."

She would be equally proud on April 7th, 1853, when her youngest son was born. This child she named after her beloved uncle Leopold. Little Leopold's birth marked a change for Victoria and, in large part, for much of the world. The queen, for the very first time, was able to ease the agonies of childbirth through the use of chloroform. Prior to this, she had suffered greatly during the births of all of her children, but with the aid of this new pain reliever, she found the experience much different. She reported, "The effect was soothing, quieting and delightful beyond measure."

However, this more peaceful experience with childbirth would be marred by the fact that Leopold had the deadly disease known as hemophilia. Hemophiliacs suffer from a condition in which their blood does not congeal properly, meaning the slightest injury could have them bleeding to death. The gene is carried in a dormant form by females, but it becomes active in males.

Thus, Victoria carried this gene, and several of her royal descendants, springing up all across Europe through later intermarriages, would end up having this dreadful condition. One of the most famous of these individuals was the little Prince Alexei, the son of the last Russian tsar, Nicholas II (Alexei was the grandson of Victoria's second-eldest daughter, Alice, making him Victoria's great-grandson). Leopold, just like his later Russian cousin, developed into a weak and often unhealthy child.

Victoria had a hard time dealing with the stress of Leopold's health problems, and her once-trained temper began to boil over as a consequence. In frustration, Albert fired off a note to his wife in which he chastised her for her childish behavior. The missive read, "Dear Child, now it will be the right to consider calmly the facts of the case. The whole offence which led to continuance of hysterics for more than an hour, and the traces of which have remained for more than 24 hours more, was: that I complained of your turning several times from inattention the wrong leaves in a Book which was to be [used] by us as a Register of prints...The miserable trifle produced the distressing scene...In which I am accused of making things worse by my false method of treatment."

Prince Albert then went on to say, "I admit that my treatment has on this occasion as on former ones signally failed, but I know of no other...When I try to demonstrate the groundlessness and injustice of the accusations which are brought against me I increase your distress...But I never intend or wish to offend you...If you are violent, I have no other choice but to leave you...I leave the room and retire to my own room in order to give you time to recover yourself. Then you follow me to renew the dispute and to have it all out."

Anyone who has ever had a few bad go-rounds with their spouse can attest to just how destructive lingering disagreements can be. You try to make peace or even walk out of a room to avoid an argument only to have your spouse close at your heels, reiterating the same frustrating points over and over again. Albert, too, seems to complain about how his wife can't seem to let a matter drop, instead choosing to keep on bringing it up.

After describing the situation as thus, Albert then clarifies his feelings. "Now don't believe that I do not sincerely and deeply pity you for the sufferings you undergo, or that I deny you do really suffer very much, I merely deny that I am the cause of them, though I have unfortunately often been the occasion...I am often astonished at the effect which a hasty word of mine has produced...In your candid way,

you generally explain later what was the real cause of your compliant...It appears now that the apprehension that you might be made answerable for the suffering of the baby (occasioned by the milk of the Wet nurse not agreeing on account of your having frequently expressed a wish to have a Nurse from the Highlands of Scotland) was the real cause of your distress which broke out on occasion of the Registration of the prints."

In this long-winded account, Albert narrates how Victoria's increasing doom and gloom over her son's health problems had caused her to blow up over nothing. They had simply been going over their routine registration prints when Victoria took all of her anxiety over her son out on poor Prince Albert. Albert was apparently fairly fed up with the treatment and even went as far as to call his thirty-four-year-old wife "a child" because of it.

Soon enough, however, international matters would distract Victoria and Albert, allowing them to forget all about any petty domestic squabbles they might be having. For in the fall of 1853, the Crimean War erupted in all of its fury. Just how the Crimean War began is not easy to explain. The most commonly cited cause is the fact that the Russian government began making demands over the rights of Orthodox Christians within lands controlled by the Ottomans—specifically the Holy Land.

Western Christian nations, such as Italy and France, were jockeying to become the champions of Catholics in the region. In the meantime, the Ottoman Empire, which had once been feared by Christian Europe as the ultimate bogeyman, had become significantly weakened, and Western powers actually came to fear what the collapse of the Ottoman Empire might bring more than the Ottomans themselves. They especially feared Russia becoming more dominant in the region. And, of course, Russia was more than ready to carve up the corpse of a dying Ottoman Empire for its own benefit.

Queen Victoria's feelings were rather ambivalent on the matter. She recorded a journal entry that read, "On such an occasion one feels wretched at being a woman though my heart is not in this unsatisfactory war." Queen Victoria was now seeing her countrymen fighting the land with which her own birth name was tied. After all, she came into this world as Alexandrina, having been named after Russian Tsar Alexander I.

As the war progressed, she listened very carefully to all the dispatches coming from the front lines. Then, a year into the fighting, she spoke with one of the men leading the struggle, a certain Lieutenant Colonel Jeffreys, who told her, in person, of "the misery, the suffering, the total lack of everything, the sickness" that the troops were facing. As the British press began to report how bad things were, Victoria began to fear that it would affect troop morale and inadvertently help Russian propaganda.

After her talk with the lieutenant colonel, she mulled over these things in her diary, writing, "He admitted that this was a great misfortune, but that on the other hand they felt certain things ought to be made known, else they would not be remedied, and the country must understand what has been going on. The trenches, badly drained, were full of water so that one had to lie up to one's waist in it. This was even the case with the Officers, who hardly had had time to change their boots, being constantly obliged to turn out in the night. What must it then have been with the poor men? They had to lie down in their wet clothes, frequently being unable to change them for 1 or 2 nights. They froze and when they did pull off their boots, portions of their feet would come off with them! This Colonel Jeffreys himself had seen and could therefore declare to be no exaggeration of the newspapers."

Victoria was deeply troubled by what the British troops were experiencing during this dreadful war. She wanted to do something to help, so she made sure to personally inspect the hospitals in which many of these wounded warriors ended up. Here, she saw men in all

sorts of horrible conditions. Some had lost feet, others hands, and still others whole arms and legs. There were also terrible diseases that the men had contracted while in the midst of warfare.

Victoria would later recall her experience of seeing these poor souls, "One could not wish the war to have continued when one looked on these brave, noble fellows, so cruelly mutilated and suffering!"

Yes, in the first phases of the war, the whole British Army was indeed suffering. The Allied forces were pushed back by the Russians in the Battle of Balaclava in October of 1854, with the British taking the brunt of the Allied casualties—numbering over twenty thousand. The Russian winter, in the meantime, was wreaking havoc on the troops. Winter storms also managed to send some thirty British transport craft to the bottom of the sea.

Due to all of these failures, the head of the War Department, Henry Pelham-Clinton, 5th Duke of Newcastle, tendered his resignation in 1855. This was followed by the resignation of Prime Minister George Hamilton-Gordon, 4th Earl of Aberdeen, shortly after. This left Foreign Secretary Henry John Temple, 3rd Viscount Palmerston (better known as simply Palmerston) in the running to become the next prime minister. Victoria did not care too much for Palmerston, whom she viewed as untrustworthy and high-handed, but in the end, she didn't have much choice.

Chapter 10 – Holding It Together

"Do not let your feelings (very natural and usual ones) of momentary irritation and discomfort be seen by others. Don't (as you so often did and do) let every little feeling be read in your face and seen in your manner."

-Queen Victoria

By 1855, the Crimean War was certainly taking its toll on the British, and the impact was most certainly felt by Queen Victoria as well. During this time, she gave a moving speech before Parliament in which tears could actually be seen welling up in her eyes. She knew the suffering that her countrymen were going through, and as their sovereign monarch, she felt their pain on a personal level.

It wasn't until the fall of 1855 that the tide finally seemed to turn for the British. For it was around this time that the queen received word that the Russian fleet had been dealt a decisive blow and that the Russian naval base of Sebastopol had been captured. Russia was essentially crippled with the capture of this strategic port, and soon the war would be all but over.

Realizing that victory was at hand, it is said that Prince Albert suddenly exclaimed, "Come and light the bonfire!" This was obviously a time for celebration. And by lighting a bonfire, everyone in

proximity was awaken to the news. It is said that those gathered broke into spontaneous cheers. They danced, shouted, shot bullets into the air, and even played a bagpipe or two. Seeing the gleeful abandon of the crowd dancing around the fire, Albert remarked that it was "a veritable witches dance." The well-wishers gave several cheers for the queen as well as her prince consort, which were followed by a few hurrahs "for the fall of Sebastopol."

In the midst of these festivities, Prince Frederick Wilhelm of Prussia (known as Emperor Frederick III), who was visiting with his mother and father, made it known that he intended to court Queen Victoria's eldest daughter, Vicky. Vicky was only fourteen years old at the time, while Frederick was in his early twenties.

Such things were not too uncommon in those days, but even so, when Frederick made it known that he would like Vicky's hand in marriage, her parents were quick to insist that the couple wait a few more years before finalizing their union. In the end, Vicky wouldn't wed Frederick until she was seventeen years of age.

From the start, the marriage was viewed as a good match. Queen Victoria herself had enthusiastically spoken of Frederick to her old uncle Leopold, gushing, "He is a dear, excellent, charming young man, whom we shall give our dear child to with perfect confidence. What pleases us greatly is to see he is really delighted with Vicky."

And as was always the case with royal matchings, more than just the feelings of the two involved in the match were taken into consideration. The political implications were also quite paramount since the marriage was viewed as providing a strong tie between Britain and Prussia. Such things seemed more important than ever in the aftermath of the Crimean War.

Still, it was hard for Queen Victoria to accept the fact that her little girl was going to soon have to grow up and leave the family as a married woman. Knowing what was in store for her, she and Albert began to treat her as an adult. One interesting aspect of this decision

to get Vicky accustomed to adulthood was the fact that Queen Victoria decided it was no longer prudent to have Vicky eat with her younger siblings but rather to sit at the dinner table with her and Albert.

Yes, Vicky was quite literally promoted from the kiddie table to the adult table. This was hard for Queen Victoria, however, because dinner with Albert was her best chance to have some alone time with her husband. Now, she had to share these moments with her daughter, whom they were attempting to give a crash course in adulthood.

In the middle of the marriage plans for Princess Vicky, Queen Victoria found herself pregnant with what would be her last child. When she discovered that she was with child in 1856, Victoria was quite amazed. The prospect of another child at her age—she was by then in her late thirties, rapidly approaching forty—seemed almost unbearable. In her distress, it was Albert who once again emerged as her comforter-in-chief.

He wrote a heartfelt letter to his suffering wife in which he stated, "I, like everyone else in the house make the most ample allowance for your state. We cannot, unhappily, bear your bodily sufferings for you—you must struggle with them alone—the moral ones are probably caused by them, but if you were rather less occupied with yourself and your feelings and took more interest in the outside world, you would find that the greatest help of all."

This last and final child of Queen Victoria was born on April 14th, 1857, just one month prior to the queen's thirty-eighth birthday. The little girl was named Beatrice Mary Victoria Feodora. Despite the use of chloroform to ease the pain, the delivery of this child was indeed a hard one. After the baby was born, her personal physician, Sir James Clark, actually warned her to make sure that this baby was the last since he knew that pregnancy complications only grew worse with age. To this recommendation, Victoria had a rather blunt response, for she is said to have asked, "Can I have no more fun in bed?"

As funny as it sounds, this was a completely candid question on the queen's part. Since this was, of course, long before birth control would be commonly available, she honestly wondered how she might continue to have intimate relations with her husband and avoid future pregnancies.

At any rate, despite the hardship of her labor, Victoria bounced back rather quickly and was even in a good mood. Just a couple of weeks later, she informed those around her about her condition, stating, "I have felt better and stronger this time, than I have ever done before. How I also thank God for granting us such a dear, pretty girl, which I so much wished for!"

She also was rather fond and affectionate with her new child. Shortly after Beatrice was born, Victoria saw the baby being given a bath and happily remarked, "A greater duck, you could not see and she is such a pet of her Papa's, stroking his face with her two dear little hands." And by the time the girl was a year old, Victoria recorded in her diary, "No words can express what that sweet, pretty, intelligent little creature is to us!"

Nevertheless, despite all of these gentle musings, Queen Victoria was known to be a rather stern parent at times. For example, she seemed to overdo the corporal punishment parents often administered to their children at the time. She once beat her often sickly son Leopold with such force that her own mother pleaded with her to cease and desist. And when asked how she could stand to hear her children cry so much, the queen retorted, "Once you've had nine, mother, you don't notice anymore."

Prince Albert, on the other hand, was known as being more lenient, and he was quite upset when his wife was hard on the kids. Albert later weighed in on the situation by writing to his wife, "It is a pity you find no consolation in the company of your children. The root of the trouble lies in the mistaken notion that the function of a mother is always to be correcting, scolding and ordering them about

and organizing their activities. It is not possible to be on happy friendly terms with people you have just been scolding."

Around this time, the so-called Indian Rebellion occurred in British India. This mutiny was actually aimed at the British East India Company. The British East India Company was essentially a trading company, which specialized in the trade of goods from East India. Although the company was not officially part of British officialdom, the British East India Company often acted as if it was an arm of the British government.

The mutiny itself was sparked by an outcry against British reforms and taxation, which put the British East India Company in the crosshairs of rioters. The bloodshed that resulted was immense. Victoria herself reflected on this fact, noting in her diary, "One's blood runs cold, and one's heart bleeds. Many have succeeded in escaping, but after unheard of sufferings and having lost all. And that this should happen after years of tranquility and security!"

Even as the mutiny was put down by British troops, Victoria was appalled at not just the trauma inflicted on the British but also the pain inflicted on the Indian rebels. She was moved to instruct British colonials to give more respect to Indian culture, religion, and vocations. She also stressed that employment opportunities must be available to native Indians just as they were available to British colonials.

Just as this latest fire within the British Empire was put out, Queen Victoria's daughter Vicky married her prince. The wedding took place in St. James's Palace at the Chapel Royal on January 25th, 1858. About a week after the marriage was confirmed, the couple then left for Berlin. The parting was a bittersweet one. Although Victoria was happy for her daughter and Vicky herself was happy to go live with Prince Frederick, both were sad to part company.

As Queen Victoria would later recall, "Still I struggled but as I came to the staircase my breaking heart gave way. Also, amongst the many servants there, I don't think there was a dry eye. Poor dear child, she kissed 1ˢᵗ one, then the other, shaking hands with many. I clasped her in my arms, not knowing what to say and kissed good Fritz, pressing his hand again and again. He was quite unable to speak for emotion. Again, at the door of the carriage I embraced them both."

Approximately one year later, on January 27ᵗʰ, 1859, Vicky would give birth to a son, who would later go on to become the infamous Kaiser Wilhelm II, who oversaw Germany's war efforts during World War I. It was a hard birth for the young woman; in fact, it was a breech birth, where the baby is born bottom first instead of head first. And during the struggle of being born, the infant Wilhelm's arm was dislocated. His left arm would remain slightly out of sync for the rest of his life.

Nevertheless, the birth of the queen's first grandchild was a joyous occasion, and it was commemorated in London with fireworks launched from Windsor Castle. And soon enough, Victoria took a keen interest in her new grandchild and how her daughter was going to raise him. Now that they were both mothers, their conversations with each other become much more intimate. In fact, they seemed to develop a greater understanding of each other. As Victoria put it in one of her diary entries at the time, "We so completely understand one another. She is a dear, clever, good affectionate child, and we are like two sisters."

Victoria was not quite so generous with her second oldest child, Albert Jr, who was better known as "Bertie" at the time. In letters Queen Victoria wrote to Vicky during this period, she bluntly described her teenage son as being both "ugly" and "dull."

In many ways, the close bond she forged with her daughter during this period mirrored the relationship that she had enjoyed with her own mother. She and her mother were the best of confidantes for

many years. And now Victoria was repaying the favor to her eldest daughter Vicky.

Actually, that very year that Victoria was forging this closeness with Vicky, Queen Victoria's own mother, the Duchess of Kent and Strathearn, began to suffer from serious health problems. When it appeared that her mother was not going to recover from this bout of illness, Victoria poured out her feelings on the matter to her old uncle Leopold, writing him, "I hardly myself knew how I loved her, or how my whole existence seems bound up with her, till I saw looming in the distance the fearful possibility of what I will not mention."

That "fearful possibility" that was "looming in the distance" arrived on March 16th, 1861. Victoria called the passing of her mother a "dreaded terrible calamity" and "an awful dream" from which she was unable to awaken.

Many who have suffered through the loss of a close loved one can relate to the feeling of being stuck in some sort of nightmare. It is the feelings of denial over what has happened and the mind's initial inability to accept the loss of someone so close that creates this dreamlike quality. One feels like they are stuck in a fog of disorientation and sadness that cannot quite be real.

But instead of her grief getting better, once she came to better accept what had happened, her grief actually appeared to grow worse, making some wonder if Britain's monarch had truly gone off the deep end. Things were so bad, in fact, that Albert often pleaded with Victoria to regain her senses. Yes, she was sad because her mother passed away, but she was still the head of state of the British Empire. She had no choice but to somehow hold it together.

Chapter 11 – Picking up the Pieces

"We placed the wreaths upon the splendid granite sarcophagus, and at its feet, and felt that only the earthly robe we loved so much was there. The pure, tender, loving spirit which loved us so tenderly, is above us—loving us, praying for us, and free from all suffering and woe. Yes, that is a comfort, and that first birthday in another world must have been a far brighter one than any in this poor world below!"

-Queen Victoria

Victoria was deeply saddened by her mother's passing, but nevertheless, her death had been somewhat expected. She was, after all, getting advanced in years and had suffered from a series of health problems. But what Victoria did not see coming was the early death of her husband Albert shortly thereafter. At this point, Albert was in his early forties, just like Queen Victoria, and although he had suffered through bouts of sickness, Victoria always figured they were just passing phases.

At times, she even considered his spells of illness to be feigned or exaggerated. She accused Albert of as much in 1861 when she wrote a letter to Vicky that stated, "Dear Papa never allows he is any better or

will try to get over it, but makes such a miserable face that people always think he's very ill. It is quite the contrary with me always; I can do anything before others and never show it, so people never believe I am ill or even suffer. His nervous system is easily excited and irritated and he's so completely overpowered by everything."

Yes, Victoria basically thought that her husband was being a big baby and pretending he was sick just to get attention. She spoke of how she was better than he was at suffering through discomfort, and she wrote off his maladies as figments of his overactive imagination. Little did she know that the husband she claimed was faking illness would die in his early forties, whereas she would get to live well into her nineties.

Interestingly enough, Albert's worsening health would end up closely tied to his son Bertie. Albert Jr, otherwise known as "Bertie," had not lived up to his parents' high expectations—a fact that they constantly reminded him of. His academic achievement was less than stellar, so his parents decided to send him off to the infantry, figuring that martial training might instill some discipline in him.

While he was at an army camp in Ireland, Bertie became acquainted with an Irish actress by the name of Nellie Clifden. Clifden apparently was known to make the rounds and "entertain the troops," and Bertie's comrades set it up so that she could personally "entertain him" in the privacy of his own tent.

To be perfectly blunt, in those days, actresses were viewed as little better than prostitutes. And Nellie Clifden was a notorious fixture at London's dance clubs, where her routine wouldn't have been all that dissimilar to a modern-day stripper. This gives you an idea of just what kind of "entertainment" she may have offered Bertie.

At any rate, one thing led to another, and the next thing Bertie knew, he was losing his virginity to this notorious actress. Such an instance probably wouldn't have been that big of a deal for any other

young man Bertie's age, but the fact that he was destined to be the future king of Britain immediately sent the gossip wheels turning.

And soon enough, word of the escapade leaked out, and all of London was talking of it. One can only imagine how mortified Bertie's mother and father were once they realized what their son had done, knowing that such scandalous details were being spread to just about every busybody on the street. Wishing to correct his son, Albert went to personally speak with him about the matter.

They ended up going for a walk together, and while engrossed in their discussion, Prince Albert didn't notice the storm clouds on the horizon. Soon, it was pouring rain, and both father and son were completely drenched as they continued their emotional dialogue. In what seems to be an eerie parallel to what had happened to Victoria's own father, this rain would lead to Prince Consort Albert's own demise. Because as soon as Albert went home to Victoria, he came down with a bad cold and a high fever that just wouldn't go away.

However, despite his sickness, on November 30th, 1861, he was able to pull off one last diplomatic act that may well have been the best save of face ever offered by the British Empire. America was in the grip of the Civil War at the time, and the Confederates of the South had been needling the British to support their cause. It is true that some in Britain may have wished to see the federal government of America suffer due to the previous animosity between the two governments.

But siding with the Confederates just to give the US federal government a hard time was an impossibility. Simply put, the British Empire, which had already abolished slavery several decades prior, was hardly going to side with a bunch of slave-holding Confederates who were seeking to reinforce the institution of slavery. Nevertheless, Confederate representatives hopped onto a British ship in order to try and persuade the British to render them aid.

When this British craft, with its Confederate passengers, was captured by Union forces, Britain found itself in a rather sticky situation. Prince Consort Albert, despite his increasing sickness, managed to carefully talk Britain out of being sucked into the American Civil War and maintain the British Empire's neutrality in the conflict. Albert was able to tactfully negotiate an agreement that would essentially allow both parties to save face and avoid war with each other.

Shortly after his masterful handling of this drama, Alfred took some powerful painkillers and laid down to rest. It was the last great act of his career, and he would die just weeks later at the age of forty-two. Victoria, of course, was beside herself with grief. She was so distraught, in fact, that she had to be given a dose of opium just to calm down.

One can only imagine the dreadful scene as the queen lay sedated in bed, in and out of consciousness, as she cried incessantly over her loss. She was so unhinged that she was unable to even attend her husband's funeral service. She never imagined that her husband would die at such a young age. She also couldn't help but blame her estranged son Bertie. After all, it was during Albert's talk with Bertie that he seemed to catch quite literally his "death of a cold."

Even if there was some truth in this (which there is), most parents would probably refuse to outright blame their child for their father's death. If the child were to cry out, "Oh, it's all my fault Daddy died!" the surviving parent would most likely reassure them by saying, "Oh honey! It's not your fault! You mustn't say that! Don't blame yourself!" Queen Victoria, on the other hand, rather openly and candidly blamed her son for his father's death, and she would continue to do so for the rest of his life.

As soon as Queen Victoria was able to regain her senses well enough to dictate to her ministers, she decreed that the entire realm should be in a period of mourning for Albert for no less than two whole years. She wanted all of Britain to grieve right along with her.

And during those two years, if anyone laughed or showed any sign of happiness in her presence, she was quick to upbraid them for it.

The queen was so distressed that some wondered if perhaps she would retire early and hand over the throne to her son Bertie. But those who speculated about such things had no idea of the enmity that Victoria felt toward her son. She loathed the idea of him being a king, and despite her pain, she decided to go on ruling for as long as she could so that she would never (at least while she was still among the living) see the day that her son ruled Great Britain.

Even though Queen Victoria decided to remain on the throne, she became a bit of a recluse after Albert's death. She no longer showed up for public events. She even avoided the wedding of her own daughter, Alice, when she married Prince Louis of Hesse-Darmstadt in the summer of 1862. Alice, for her part, was no doubt sick of all the grieving in the home and eager to get out of that dark house of mourning as soon as possible.

When Bertie himself got married the following year in 1863 to the Danish Princess Alexandra, Queen Victoria found a more inventive way to avoid others. Instead of skipping out on the event entirely, she actually hid herself up "in a closet high above the altar of St. George's Chapel." That way, she could peer out at the wedding procession without anyone being the wiser.

After the wedding, she returned to her quarters unnoticed, where she shared a quiet meal with her five-year-old daughter Beatrice. The journal entry Victoria made shortly thereafter was full of melancholy, but it also included some positive overtures for the future. She wrote, "Here I sit lonely and desolate, who so need love and tenderness, while our two daughters have each their loving husbands and Bertie has taken his lovely pure sweet bride to Osborne. Such a jewel whom he is indeed lucky to have obtained. How I pray God may ever bless them!"

This melancholic scrawl was probably the most positive face that Victoria could put on in light of the pain, heartache, and disappointment that she so deeply felt. Bertie and his new wife Alexandra had a son (Albert Victor) in 1864, and for a time, Victoria, who was often a doting grandmother, appeared to ease up on her hostility toward Bertie.

She also managed to find a positive outlet for some of her grief. During this time, she often rallied the cause of widows. This was perhaps most dramatically demonstrated in 1865 when she fired off a heartfelt letter to the recently widowed wife of US President Abraham Lincoln. After Lincoln's assassination, Queen Victoria sent an official missive to Lincoln's wife, Mary, which stated, in part, "Though a stranger to you I cannot remain silent when so terrible a calamity has fallen upon you and your country and must personally express my deep and heartfelt sympathy with you under the chocking circumstances of your present dreadful misfortune. No one can better appreciate than I can, who am myself utterly broken-hearted by the loss of my own beloved husband, who was the light of my life—my stay, my all—what your sufferings must be. And I earnestly pray that you may be supported by Him to whom alone the sorely stricken can look for comfort, in this hour of heavy affliction."

Like many world leaders under similar circumstances, her own personal hardship had created in her a sense of sympathy for the downtrodden, the weak, the widowed, and the less fortunate. It was not until 1866 that the queen returned to much of her public duties, attending Parliament for the first time since Albert's death in February of 1866 and holding official court proceedings by the following summer. That year, she also managed to marry off her daughter Helena, who was wed to Prince Christian of Schleswig-Holstein.

During her time of hardship, Queen Victoria crafted a close relationship with a man named John Brown. Brown was a hired hand at one of the queen's estates in Scotland. The man was a devoted servant, but he had become quite friendly with the queen. Queen

Victoria enjoyed Brown's light-hearted nature and spoke very highly of him. At one point, she noted in her diary, "He [John Brown] is so devoted to me—so simple, so intelligent, so unlike an ordinary servant, and so cheerful and attentive."

In Victoria's later years, she and Brown would indeed become inseparable, leading some to gossip that there was perhaps even more to their relationship than anyone else fully realized. The exact nature of Brown and Victoria's relationship is still hotly debated by historians. But not to get too bogged down in the details, what one can state without much question is that these two certainly enjoyed one another's company.

In John Brown, the queen had not only a loyal servant but also a best friend. She herself once referred to Brown as "her heart's best treasure." So, at least in an emotional sense, it is pretty clear that Brown eventually filled in as a surrogate for the late Prince Albert. This did not go well with much of the public, who wondered what the queen was off doing with this Scotsman, who was drunk much of the time.

Brown's closeness to the queen made members of Parliament rather unhappy, too, in the knowledge that their sovereign might be influenced by this man whom they knew very little about. Just what was the queen telling this strange man when the two would go out alone in secluded areas while riding horses? These were the concerns that kept some members of Parliament up at night.

Fears that she might be feeding state secrets to her Scottish lover were indeed on the menu in those days. Some of the more frustrated even mocked the queen behind her back, referring to her as "Mrs. Brown." Things came to a head in 1868 when members of Parliament sought to issue an injunction that prevented the queen from publicly appearing with John Brown.

It was actually the queen's own personal physician who intervened on Victoria's behalf. Her doctor bluntly informed those who wished to take Brown from her that without Brown, she "might go mad." Brown also proved invaluable as the queen's protector. This was fully displayed on February 29th, 1872, when a quick-acting Brown possibly saved the queen's very life.

On that day, a seventeen-year-old troublemaker by the name of Arthur O'Connor trespassed onto the grounds of Buckingham Palace with ill intent toward the queen. Queen Victoria, who was accompanied by Brown, arrived in a horse-drawn carriage shortly thereafter. The next thing Victoria knew, a strange figure (Arthur O'Connor) was shoving his face right into hers through the window of her carriage. It was very similar to what had happened to Prince Albert several years before.

But unlike Prince Albert, the queen's current companion was a man of action. Rather than taking this abuse lying down, Brown leaped upon the interloper, and after a thrashing, he pinned the young man down in a viselike grip until the police arrived to arrest him. It was later discovered that the man had a gun and that he likely intended to use it against the queen. John Brown, like some Scottish, kilt-wearing (yes, he enjoyed wearing kilts) superhero, had leaped to action and saved the day. Yes, in many ways, it was the loving kindness of good old John Brown that was keeping the queen going during this dark period of her life.

The queen herself later remarked to her eldest daughter Vicky about the matter, stating, "When one's beloved husband is gone and one's children are married—one feels that a friend who can devote him or herself entirely to you is the one thing you do require to help you on—and to sympathize entirely with you. Not that you love your children less—but you feel as they grow up and marry that you can be of so little use to them, and they to you." And when Brown eventually passed away in 1883, this great friend would be sorely missed.

Chapter 12 – The Later Years

"There are long periods when life seems a small, dull round, a petty business with no point, and then suddenly we are caught up in some great event which gives us a glimpse of the solid and durable foundations of our existence."

-Queen Elizabeth II

The last few decades of the 19th century seemed to go by at a rapid clip for Queen Victoria. The year 1867 saw a rare expedition launched to the East African nation of Ethiopia. Back then, the borders of Ethiopia covered more ground, and the region was referred to as an empire. It was ruled by a long line of emperors who were said to have descended from the Queen of Sheba and King Solomon of the Bible.

In 1867, the Ethiopian emperor who sat on the throne was a man named Tewodros II, but the English usually referred to him as "Theodore." Tewodros had been attempting to enter into more open relations with Britain, and he was especially seeking military assistance from the British. Ethiopia was facing aggression from Egypt at the time, and Tewodros felt that since Ethiopia was a Christian nation, it was only natural that their Christian brothers in England would help them against Muslim aggressors from Egypt.

He was enraged and infuriated, however, when Britain decided to side with Egypt instead. Tewodros failed to realize that by the late 19th century, Britain's economic interests usually trumped its religious interests. And while religious crusades may have been appealing to the British in the days of Richard the Lionheart in the 12th century, by the late 1800s, Britain's monetary interests typically reigned supreme. And Egypt was simply more strategically important for these interests.

Tewodros II did not take this rejection very well. In his anger, he took several Europeans as hostages. As absurd as it sounds, he concocted a scheme to try and force the more technical-minded among his hostages to fashion firearms for him. You see, Ethiopia at that time had a limited supply of guns and did not possess its own means to produce them.

The fact that Tewodros would seize random Europeans who just happened to be in his country and try and force them to build guns for him is outrageous, but Ethiopia was in a desperate situation. Nevertheless, the plan backfired on him big time when England sent a full-fledged expeditionary force to free the hostages.

Tewodros himself had more than a few screws loose, and he had already upset most of his own subjects. As such, when the British made it clear to average Ethiopians that their mission was not one to conquer Ethiopia but rather to just free the hostages and take out Tewodros, the British were virtually welcomed with open arms.

Tewodros, at this point, was largely viewed as a despicable despot by his own people. His authoritarian rule and, in particular, his aggression against Ethiopian church clergy had made him decidedly unpopular. Tewodros had issued taxes against the Ethiopian Orthodox Church and had even seized church property. Such moves created great opposition against Tewodros, and his public support had greatly declined. As such, the British had no trouble storming his compound, a feat that occurred on April 13th, 1868.

The only thing that saved the Ethiopian emperor from being dragged off to England in chains was the fact that he ended his own life. Yes, just as the British were kicking down his door, he picked up a gun (ironically, the very piece of equipment he was so desperately seeking) and shot himself in the head. Keeping their word, the British then quickly departed Ethiopia (although not without looting Tewodros's compound), allowing the Ethiopians to install a new emperor: Tekle Giyorgis II.

It would later be learned that Tewodros had written personal letters to Queen Victoria stating his objectives. But the queen had never received them since they were filed away by her foreign ministry office and never shown to her. It has even been said that since they were written in Amharic script—the official language of Ethiopia—that no one was familiar enough with it at the time to translate it, so no one even bothered to inform the queen.

But nevertheless, the queen would become involved with the legacy of Tewodros in another very important way, as she would come to know the deposed emperor's son—Prince Alemayehu—who was essentially adopted by the British Army after the death of both of his parents. Although there is still some debate on this, the prince was supposedly taken into British custody for his own protection since rival Ethiopian factions were threatening to have him killed.

At any rate, British General Charles Napier charged a man called Captain Tristram Speedy with watching over the child. Captain Speedy (you have to love that name!) had been in Ethiopia before, and he was one of the few who actually spoke decent Amharic. The two are said to have developed a surprising bond. And it was a bond that Queen Victoria herself would recognize when Speedy presented the Ethiopian prince to her at her home on the Isle of Wight.

Thinking it would be best for the child, Queen Victoria arranged for Speedy and his wife to officially make Alemayehu their ward, with the British government paying for all of his expenses. Alemayehu, despite the obvious social difficulties of Victorian England, is said to

have actually done quite well for himself. He had plenty of friends, and he was a favorite on the rugby team.

He also had a powerful benefactor since the queen herself would periodically check in on his progress. Sadly enough, however, what the Ethiopian prince's ultimate future might have been remains unknown, for he contracted a terrible case of pleurisy (severe inflammation of the lungs) and passed away at just eighteen years of age. Queen Victoria saw to it that he had a proper burial and had him interred at St. George's Chapel in Windsor Castle.

While all of this international intrigue was afoot, Victoria's own family life continued to evolve. Her children were all but grown, and one after the other began to leave home. Her daughter Louise, whom she had often fretted over, finally found a match in John Campbell, 9ᵗʰ Duke of Argyll, whom she married in 1871. Next up was her son Arthur, who married Princess Louise Margaret of Prussia in 1879.

Just a few years later, Queen Victoria was able to delight in the marriage of her youngest son Leopold to Helen of Waldeck and Pyrmont in 1882. In the midst of all of these marriages, Victoria's daughter Alice abruptly perished in 1878. She died during an outbreak of diphtheria. And the fact that she died on December 14ᵗʰ— the very same day that her father had passed—was certainly not missed by Queen Victoria.

She recoiled at the cruel coincidence, declaring, "That this dear, talented, distinguished, tender hearted, noble minded sweet child, who behaved so admirably, during her dear father's illness, and afterwards, in supporting me, and helping me in every possible way— should be called back to her father, on this very anniversary, seems almost incredible, and most mysterious!"

Sadly, Alice's brother Leopold, a known hemophiliac, would be the next of Victoria's children to die. In 1884, after just two years of marriage, Leopold would suffer a fall. He hit his head, and due to complications from his hemophilia, he would die from internal

bleeding. He was just thirty years old at the time of his passing, and he left behind his widowed wife and two children.

Nevertheless, now no stranger to sorrow and loss, Queen Victoria rather stoically proclaimed, "I will labor on as long as I can for the sake of my children and for the good of the country I love so well." In reality, she was rising to the challenge of a greater cause, for she knew the turbulent tides that the world was facing, and she knew that the British Empire needed a stable steward at the helm.

In particular, she was concerned with the troubles that were brewing in the British possessions of Egypt and Sudan. In Sudan, a radical by the name of Muhammad had declared himself the great Mahdi—a religious/political figure prophesied by some Muslims—and declared that those who followed him would throw off the British yoke of imperialism.

As this rebellion gained popular support and the rebels marched on Egypt, the British initially found themselves at a loss as to what they should do. Some wanted to immediately go on the offensive, but others felt that battling such rabble-rousers wasn't even worth their time. Others took a more pragmatic approach and figured that the best policy would be one of containment. They should keep the Sudanese rebels out of Egypt but should not bother to put down the rebellion going on in Sudan.

The queen, however, would have the last say, and she decided it was time to go on the offensive. The queen was by no means a war hawk, but her intuition told her that the only way to root out this mayhem was to strike fast and to strike hard so that the Sudanese would quickly rethink taking up arms against British positions.

Nevertheless, not all of her ministers saw eye to eye with the queen on this. Some still held out hope that some sort of negotiation could be reached with the Mahdi leader. As such, a certain General Charles George Gordon was dispatched under the belief that he could persuade the rebels to stand down. General Gordon and the small

group who accompanied him, however, ended up as prisoners in Khartoum. Yet, still, the ministers dithered. And by the time British armed forces were finally sent to Khartoum to try and rescue General Gordon, they were too late.

The city had been laid waste, and they discovered General Gordon had already been killed. Queen Victoria felt terrible about the whole ordeal and even wrote a note of sympathy to the murdered general's sister. The missive read, in part, "How shall I write to you, or how shall I attempt to express what I feel! To think of your dear, noble, heroic brother, who served his country and his Queen so truly, so heroically, with a self-sacrifice so edifying to the world, not having been rescued! That the promises of support were not fulfilled—which I so frequently and constantly pressed on those who asked him to go— is to me grief inexpressible."

Nevertheless, the queen had to put on a brave face, both for her country as well as her family. For shortly after this whole debacle, her youngest child (who was twenty-seven at the time), Princess Beatrice, was set to marry Prince Henry of Battenberg. The two were wed in 1885 on the Isle of Wight.

This small, laidback community was not used to the spectacle of a royal wedding, and the local people were delighted at the fanfare that such an event brought. It is said that the residents enjoyed a kind of national holiday, in which they enjoyed music, feasts, fireworks, and all kinds of ceremonial displays. These celebrations would dovetail with the even grander showing for the queen's Golden Jubilee. A Golden Jubilee takes place on a ruling monarch's fiftieth anniversary, with Queen Victoria's occurring on June 20th, 1887.

All throughout the British Empire, there was a desire to commemorate this incredible event. There was a sudden rush to create monuments of all kinds to Queen Victoria, and suddenly the lyrics to "God Save the Queen" were on everyone's lips. During the grand celebration in Westminster Abbey, the queen was escorted into the building by an extravagant entourage that included a few of her

own sons, some sons-in-law, grandchildren, and several other various royals. These guests of honor were sure to dress in their royal best, but the queen herself was dressed all in black as if she were at a funeral rather than a jubilatory celebration. The only extravagance she allowed on her person was a bonnet, which was trimmed with white lace and diamonds.

The entourage was surrounded by well-wishers who cheered them on as they entered the abbey. After the festivities came to a close, the queen summed up her complicated feelings of the event when she wrote, "It has shown that the labour and anxiety of fifty long years, twenty-two of which I spent in unclouded happiness, shared and cheered by my beloved husband, while an equal number were full of sorrows and trials, borne without his sheltering arm and wise help, have been appreciated by my people."

Queen Victoria was indeed pleased and reassured to see that "her people" still supported her. Despite the occasional attacks against her through the years (both in the press and from actual assailants), the majority of her subjects still appeared to revere her after fifty years' worth of rule.

Toward the end of Queen Victoria's reign, her British subjects grew increasingly sentimental for the queen's reign. She had been in power for about as long as most could remember. The large part of an entire century had seen her ruling over Britain, and these feelings of sentimentality were mixed with a feeling that surely this moment wouldn't last much longer.

Sensing that the queen's time was probably short, it seems that England was making the most of the queen's remaining years. She had her Golden Jubilee in 1887, and in 1891, the marker for what would have been her fiftieth anniversary of being married to Prince Albert was commemorated, which would have been their golden wedding anniversary. The remembrance of her long-dead Albert, of course, was bittersweet, and it would bring up unpleasant memories and emotions on the part of the queen.

Then, in 1897, the queen would celebrate her Diamond Jubilee, which recognized her sixty years of reigning as the queen of Great Britain. This feat was not accomplished again until Queen Elizabeth II reached this milestone in 2012. Elizabeth II, by the way, has since surpassed all of this by celebrating her Sapphire Jubilee (sixty-five years of being queen) in 2017. It is possible she might even live to see her Platinum Jubilee (seventy years of being queen), which will be reached in 2022.

Nevertheless, during Queen Victoria's day, such longevity was hardly heard of. Most of the kings and queens who reigned during her first few years as queen were long gone, yet she was still there. Her Diamond Jubilee was celebrated with great fanfare, but the queen worried about a recent economic downturn in the British economy, so she made sure that the festivities didn't break the bank.

She managed to get a little help with financing, however, in the form of rich British subjects, such as Sir Thomas Lipton (of Lipton Tea fame), who forked out his own money to host massive tea parties for the public. All of Victoria's surviving children made sure that they attended and showed their support for her Diamond Jubilee.

All celebrations aside, the next major challenge that the queen would face during her tenure was the outbreak of the Second Boer War, which had erupted in the fall of 1899. Victoria was allegedly greatly moved by the hardships that her troops were facing, and despite her advanced age, she took it upon herself to be personally involved with the war effort.

She would oversee the training of troops, hand out medals, and go to visit those who were sent home sick and injured. Victoria began to become greatly dismayed and heartbroken over the toll that this latest conflict was taking on the empire, but by 1900, the British were able to secure peace. The price of this peace was high, however, since it only came after the loss of over 100,000 troops and expenditure in what would amount to billions of dollars in modern times.

The war seemed to have taken a personal toll on the queen, and by the following year, her own health began to go into decline. One of her journal entries from January 1st, 1901, seems to say it all when she remarked, "Another year begun—I am feeling so weak and unwell, that I enter upon it sadly."

Victoria had long grown weary of the monotony of the years. A part of her had died with Albert all those years ago. Yet, she continued to live. Now, however, her own health was beginning to decline, and she began to ponder the fact that it might all come to an end soon. She eventually became bedridden, and she finally passed away on January 22nd, 1901, at the age of eighty-one.

Conclusion: Missing the Queen

For all of the impact that she had made upon the world, in many ways, Queen Victoria could be seen as a sort of accidental monarch. For it was indeed a very rare set of circumstances that afforded her arrival to the throne in the first place. In British royalty, the male heir always took precedent over a female one. This fact alone makes female monarchs more of a rarity.

Victoria's grandfather, George III, had plenty of sons to take the throne. But none of these sons had male heirs. And after each of George's sons took turns in power, each dying one after the other, it just so happened that Victoria—George III's only legitimate surviving granddaughter—inherited the crown.

Despite the rarity of her position, Queen Victoria didn't waste any time in showing that she was in charge. Many of her ministers may have thought that they could bully and pressure Victoria into doing their bidding, but the Bedchamber Plot proved to them that they could not. This is, of course, in reference to the stand that she took early on when the candidate for prime minister tried to have her own personal attendants dismissed simply because they were married to men of the political party that had just lost favor in Parliament. Although Victoria was widely ridiculed for the move, it was at least

admirable that she was able to summon the courage and strength to stand her ground.

Shortly after this incident, she reached out to her first cousin Albert for the love and support that she so desperately craved. Prince Albert, for his part, readily gave it and married her, becoming her prince consort. Victoria then fought to elevate the status of her beloved husband, even asking Parliament to change his title to king consort. This proved to be a losing battle, but Victoria never ceased singing the praises of her husband. Even after he died in 1861, she lived the rest of her life as if she were in mourning of this man whom she so dearly loved.

All of the children that came from this union, in the meantime, grew up and married royals from other nations. They themselves then had children, adding to the various royal bloodlines of Europe. Since so many of her descendants came to populate the royal families of Europe, Queen Victoria herself would become known as the "Grandmother of Europe." She would also be known as the source of much of European royalty's hemophilia.

This dreaded disease, which causes folks to bleed to death at the slightest provocation, had first been brought to her attention when her son Leopold was diagnosed with it. Leopold would end up dying from this disease when a slight fall caused him to bleed internally, resulting in a deadly brain hemorrhage.

Despite the hardships that her family members experienced, the queen was always a strong force in England and abroad. In her later years, she would be celebrated with first a Golden Jubilee and then a Diamond one. And in her last days, she would find herself whipped up to a patriotic fervor for British troops fighting in the Second Boer war. She was most certainly one of a kind. And both her quick wit, her kind heart, and her decisive leadership would be sorely missed.

Here's another book by Captivating History that you might like

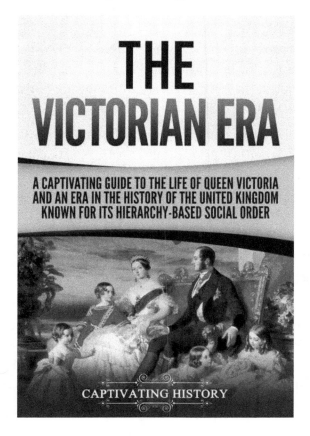

Free Bonus from Captivating History (Available for a Limited time)

Hi History Lovers!

Now you have a chance to join our exclusive history list so you can get your first history ebook for free as well as discounts and a potential to get more history books for free! Simply visit the link below to join.

Captivatinghistory.com/ebook

Also, make sure to follow us on Facebook, Twitter and Youtube by searching for Captivating History.

Appendix A: Further Reading and Reference

In the Days of Queen Victoria. Eva March Tappan. 2011.

Queen Victoria: Scenes and Incidents of Her Life and Reign. G. A. Henty. 2017.

Victoria: The Queen: An Intimate Biography of the Woman who Ruled an Empire. Julia Baird. 2016.

Queen Victoria in Her Letters and Journals. Christopher Hibbert. 2000.

The Letters of Queen Victoria: A Selection from Her Majesty's Correspondence between the Years 1837 and 1861 Volume 1, 1837–1843. Queen Victoria (edited by Reginald Baliol Brett Esher and Arthur Christopher Benson). 2011.

MW00332402